THE REAL
DOG YOGA

Jo-Rosie Haffenden

First published in 2015 by First Stone Publishing
St. Martin's Farm, Zeals, Warminster, BA12 6NZ, United Kingdom.

www.dogbooksonline.co.uk

© 2015 First Stone Publishing

ISBN
978-1-910488-17-1
1-910488-17-8

Printed by Printworks Global Ltd., London & Hong Kong

Author's Dedication

For Archie, my muse.

For Ella, my princess.

For mum and dad, my guiding lights.

For David, my inspiration.

With thanks to Ry and Claire for helping me on my journey;

Ethan and Faith for being so awesome; and to Hanna, Rach and Amy for

all your constant support.

Photography: John Daniels.

CONTENTS

FOREWORD

I have had the pleasure of knowing Jo-Rosie Haffenden and her stunning, exempt Pit Bull Terrier, Archie, for some time and we have exchanged thoughts and ideas over the years. When Jo-Rosie asked me to write this Foreword, I jumped at the chance to get a sneak preview of what I knew would be a great book.

I thought that I would be able to write my contribution within a matter of days of receiving the copy – but I was wrong. This book had me entranced from the moment I started reading the first paragraph. I found myself utterly absorbed, and my excitement grew as I read each beautifully constructed page. I couldn't put it down and I have struggled to find words that will do this book the justice it deserves.

As someone who also works with dogs, I really value the importance of advancing the education of our canine friends with quiet, non-invasive techniques that encourage fluid, balanced movement, release habitual patterns of bracing, and engages the parasympathetic nervous system where learning can occur. Every section of this stunning publication resonated with me. It is utterly brilliant, thought provoking and so refreshing to read.

Jo-Rosie recognises the inextricable link between posture and behaviour, and understands and appreciates how dogs learn.

She shares her wealth of experience in a way that will inspire and encourage dog guardians to discover the true potential of their canine companions through mindful connections that will bring far reaching benefits and rich rewards. Her book will help create serenity in a busy world and will enable carers to establish a calm, peaceful and harmonious relationship with their four-legged friends, based on deep understanding, patience, respect and utter joy.

Dog Yoga is not about 'training' nor is it about forcing a dog to participate in pointless and/or potentially stressful activities for personal gain. It is about education and teaching good life-skills that will benefit every dog, regardless of their age or experience. It reminds guardians to look for and acknowledge possibility, and liberates humans and dogs alike from limitation.

This is an exceptional book that will add new dimensions to existing knowledge regardless of the skill sets already in place, and one that honours that glorious, forgiving and tolerant being, the dog.

Sarah Fisher.

Sarah Fisher is a TTouch Instructor and behaviour counsellor. She trained with Linda Tellington Jones and Robyn Hood and organises the TTouch trainings for the UK. She has worked with animals for over 17 years and teaches staff workshops for many of the UK's top animal shelters including Battersea Dogs and Cats Home, the Mayhew Animal Home, Blue Cross, Wood Green Animal Shelter and Dogs Trust. She lectures and holds workshops in the UK and overseas and is a regular teacher on the Dogs Trust International Training Programme.

Sarah is the author of *Unlock Your Dog's Potential* and co-author of *100 Ways to Train the Perfect Dog* and *100 Ways to Solve Your Dog's Problems* with Marie Miller which have been translated into several languages.

5

ABOUT THE DOGS

MARLEY

Marley was rescued by his owners at six months. He is a Rottweiler cross breed. Unfortunately Marley had problems with guarding spaces and he was fear aggressive towards some new people. Marley uses Dog Yoga to de-escalate when he feels stressed and it has reduced this fear of new people, which means he no longer feels the need to guard.

NORA

Nora was brought home at eight weeks old as an adorable Border Terrier puppy. Nora loves her doting owner a lot and had some attachment issues which lead to separation anxiety. She now has a dog walker who ensures she gets what she needs and uses Dog Yoga to destress so that when she is left, she is chilled out.

ALFIE

Alfie is a tenacious little Chihuahua mix. He was bought home at eight weeks old but sadly a bad experience with some other dogs meant that he suffered with anxieties around new dogs. Dog Yoga helped Alfie enter situations around other dogs at a lower state and gave him a way to self-soothe when he felt anxious. His owner also reports that he has increased the amount of appeasement gestures he uses around other dogs when he feels stressed now since she put them on cue.

BUBBLES

Bubbles is a Kooikerhondje cross and she was rescued at 12 months after being bred very early and left in a crate with her puppies. Bubbles is a very anxious little dog but very smart too! She has fear and anxiety issues around other dogs and new people. She also finds new situations and places hard to deal with. Her owner has used Dog Yoga to reduce anxiety in new situations and around new doggy friends.

LILY

Lily was a rescue Saluki x Greyhound who found her home at 11 weeks. Lily is generally very chilled out and relaxed. She has no behaviour issues but at 11 years old she does suffer with some stiffness. Lily's owner has found practising Dog Yoga loosens her joints and allows her to remain in top shape!

RALPH

Ralph is an American Bulldog cross who was rescued out of the pound. He suffers with frustration problems and used to guard his resources as well.

Ralph has also suffered with significant health complaints since arriving at his new home which has meant that he has had to be walked on a lead and, at times, had very little exercise. His owner uses Dog Yoga to keep him mentally stimulated and generally out of trouble!

BENJI

Benji is a 16-week-old Staffordshire Bull Terrier cross. He is only just learning Dog Yoga to combat a few minor anxiety issues he has had since arriving from a rescue centre.

JACKSON

Jackson is a working Collie who lives in a domestic home. Jackson is very smart and needs extra stimulation to ensure that his needs are being met. Jack

sometimes works on TV too and has starred on *Good Morning, Fool Britannia* and in various magazines. We are always looking for things to ensure that Jack is kept mentally stimulated and Dog Yoga also helps him to deal with stressful new situations.

ELLA

Ella is a very energetic Hungarian Vizsla. She is smart but can get very frustrated. As a result of her drivey nature and her frustration, as well as the fact that she is only 11 months, Ella has little impulse control. We have used Dog Yoga to teach Ella to be calm at home and to help her focus and control those strong urges that sometimes lead to mischief!

ARCHIE

Archie is a registered Pit Bull Terrier who sadly had his ears cut off when he was a puppy. Archie came to me at six months and suffered with extreme frustration and anxiety. Archie inspired the whole method of Dog Yoga as he found the pressure of conventional training too much to handle. Dog Yoga has changed Archie's life and he is now able to live happily with Ella and the cat as well as enjoy meeting new people and going to exciting new places!

INTRODUCTION

Patience is a virtue; in dog training, it is essential. The vast majority of tasks related to living with dogs are rushed. Many of the common training problems would be reduced, or even resolved, if we simply doubled the time we took to do everything with our dogs.

If you have a dog your first lesson is to sit, in silence, and watch your dog for 30 minutes. Your second lesson is to sit at your local park or field and to watch your dog for another 30 minutes in silence. Arguably you will learn more in this hour than you will in any hour-long training class. First of all learn to be still and quiet around your dog: to be invisible. Watch, listen and see how your dog negotiates with his domestic world without interference.

The 'uncared block' in Taoism (which is translated from the Chinese 'Pu') refers to a state of pure potential. The condition of the mind before the interference of force. Our dogs begin their lives, as we do, as uncared blocks. We must study who they are, and then begin to help them shape and reach their potential in the right way which works with, as opposed to against, nature – and without force.

The image of dogs doing hand stands and crossing their paws is indeed a comical one, but it is actually with spiritual, mental and physical goals in mind that we look at Yoga for dogs. In teaching, this discipline looks more like a mix of the competitive equestrian sport dressage, canine obedience and animal trick training.

There has been an unhealthy trend of people doing human Yoga with their dogs. This practice, coined Doga is an unfortunate fashion. The classes are usually held by Yoga practitioners with the general public bringing domestic dogs into the space. The idea is that the dogs stay on the mat with their owner and are incorporated into specific poses. Doga tends to be geared towards smaller breeds and most of the classes I have witnessed are packed with mini dogs who are easier to handle. The practice involves:

• The owner holding his dog into the air, often with the backend unsupported.
• Pinning the dog on to his back with the owner's body over them.
• Propping the dog on the owner's back. where the dog is forced to balance if he can't jump off.

The practice has nothing to do with providing dogs with any of the benefits associated with either the physical or spiritual practice of real Yoga and is simply a forceful practice which demeans dogs and dupes owners into believing they are providing their dog with something that reduces stress when, in fact, the opposite is true. Conventional Yoga can be defined as "the stilling of the changing states of the mind". The term 'Yoga' first appeared in the Hindu scripture Katha Upanishad and it referred to attaining a steady control of the senses. However, in the contemporary Western world, Yoga is considered more as a complete exercise programme than the route to a supreme state. But as anyone who has practised Yoga will agree, the benefits are not only physical but spiritual, too. Practising Yoga helps to alleviate health problems, improve muscle control, reduce stress and improve positive body consciousness.

In 1872 Charles Darwin first posed the idea that emotional responses influence how we feel. He wrote: "The free expression by outward signs of an emotion intensifies it". The scientific community appreciates this theory and it is clear that the expression of an emotion drives behaviour – with more intense emotional responses driving more intense behaviours.

In recent times, we have had the technology which enables us to look inside the canine waking brain to explore what is going on inside that mysterious black box. MRI studies of dogs who were trained to go into the MRI machines voluntarily and to stay in there, awake, have revealed many exciting, if slightly predictable results. When looking at

Unlike in 'Doga' dogs taking part in the Real Dog Yoga choose to partake in the postures which enhance the human-dog bond.

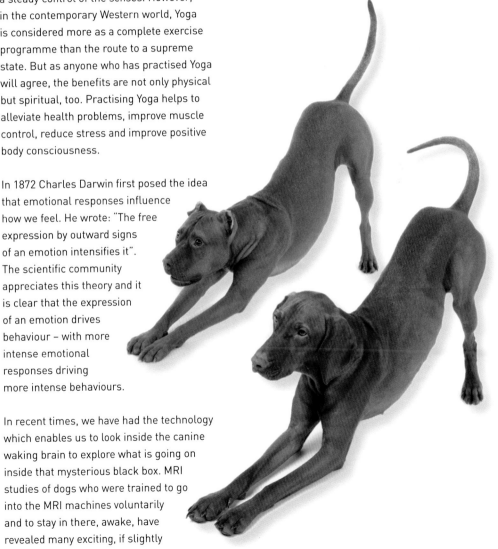

9

the human brain we can use the activity of the caudate nucleus to predict preference. Gregory Berns, professor of neuroeconomics at Emory University, found that the same seems true of dogs. When a hand signal indicates that food is coming, or when an owner returns into the room with the dog, activity in this part of the brain is also indicative of positive feelings. Additionally we can measure the level of hormones such as oxytocin, released when we feel love. Oxytocin is also released in dogs which leads us to believe that dogs do, indeed, feel love and are aware of being loved.

Psychologists at the University of Cardiff in Wales considered the idea that our physical expressions affect our emotions. Their research revealed that people whose ability to frown is compromised by cosmetic Botox injections are happier, on average, than people who are able to frown. The idea that not only the environment, but physical posturing and expressions can influence our emotional state is something I have observed in dogs over the 29 years I have spent in their company.

We have seen that canids, like many mammalian species, predominately communicate using a variety of body postures. Like humans smiling and frowning, these postures seem to stimulate the parasympathetic nervous system (that's the one that releases the happy, positive and calming chemicals associated with the process of rest/digest and feed/breed).

Dog Yoga sets out to train sequences of these positive and calming postures, which are then practiced in a sequence to promote good mental, physical and emotional health and, importantly, calmness.

In traditional dressage, horses display a predetermined range of impressive movements which not only look beautiful, but also show incredible muscle control and often an admirable dialogue between horse and rider. In the world of dog sports, we have doggy dancing (canine freestyle/heelwork to music), but this is not at all the same as dressage. Doggy dancing shows discipline and high levels of training, but it is highly arousing, often frustrating, and does nothing to reinforce calmness or sensual control, which is what yoga does for people, and what dressage can do for horses.

There is no reason why dogs cannot feel the benefits of stillness training, as we do when we practise Yoga. This cannot, however, be achieved by ignorant people forcing dogs into unnatural postures and positions; it must be practised with the upmost respect and appreciation for the dog as a sentient being.

There are 84 asanas in classical human yoga. In Real Dog Yoga there are 30 postures, 15 expressions and 10 actions. There are more advance postures, but this book sets out to train dogs in muscle control, body consciousness, focus of the mind and also impulse control. These basic practices set out to reduce stress, increase agility, flexibility and promote good mental and physical health. It can also significantly improve the human-dog connection and create a dialogue between owner and dog via an empowered, calm and optional type of *force-free* learning.

Ella performs a bow which stretches her back, increases her body awareness and teaches her to be friendly.

Archie learns to cross his paws on cue which fine tunes his ability to listen to his caregiver and perform accurate behaviours.

WHY TRAIN DOGS YOGA?

Our western expectation of the domestic dog has never been higher. We expect our dogs to get on with every dog, cat, baby and person they meet; alert us when strangers come to the house but not bark at the postman. We expect them to walk perfectly on a lead, come when called, sniff when we ask but ignore potent scent where another dog has marked if we are in a rush. We want our domestic dogs to be calm and not demanding but also playful when we want, and to only chew the things we give them. All this is expected from a species whose survival was based on scavenging, anticipating threats and danger through scent, keeping their teeth sharp by chewing, and living in a social group based on the quiet, slow negotiation of space.

To a dog, a lead, for example, is arbitrary: for that matter so is a puppy pad, a clicker, a sofa and the word "sit" – and yet there is a huge human expectation that dogs will understand these items, materials and words. I am not suggesting that we have to lower our expectations for this wise, emotionally intelligent and highly adaptable species. But we do owe it to our canine companions to, at least, give them a clue as to what it is we want from them, and to spend some time listening.

Dogs communicate constantly through their body language.

While they may not talk; dogs are speaking all the time.

PUPPIES

Traditionally we take on a puppy at around seven to eight weeks of age from a wide variety of sources. More recently there have been media campaigns showing the results of bad breeding on the physical attributes of dogs. Less emphasis has been placed on the significant effect that poor breeding can have on temperament and behaviour.

The responsible prospective puppy owner will research a breed and a breeder. They will take the time to meet both parents before they pick their puppy, and will ensure that their puppy's breeder has exposed the litter in a positive way to situations they will encounter throughout their lives, such as other species, novel items, and people of all ages.

Backyard breeders and puppy farmers breed for money and do not have the best interest of the puppies in mind. They breed one dog with another dog, regardless of temperament or behaviour. These puppies may be predisposed genetically (with some behaviours having a genetic component) to specific behaviours or emotional states.

Additionally, and perhaps more significantly, puppies learn postures and reactions from their parents (allelomimic behaviour – mimicking, as well as social facilitation – where the presence of more dogs creates an increase in the intensity of behaviour, have both been consistently observed in scientific study). Fear, anxiety and frustration is far more prevalent in dogs kept in inappropriate conditions. All these very early learning experiences affect the puppy that comes home to live in our domestic setting, and it is important to bear in mind that some puppies are born with a much higher likelihood of displaying certain behavioural traits. However, we take puppies home at the tender age of seven weeks and expect them to adapt to our lives – in many cases, this is regardless of poor early conditions. Puppies learn about the world around them from birth but with positive and patient care giving, a worried, scared or under exposed puppy can be turned around.

Benji is a 16-week-old Staffordshire Bull Terrier cross. He is learning Real Dog Yoga to combat minor anxiety issues.

From the moment we take a puppy home, he starts to learn about his new life as a pet dog: what is scary and what serves to provide functional rewards. Socialisation, both in terms of environment, other creatures, different materials (getting puppies used to traffic cones, bin bags, high heels and other such strange human things) is something now widely practised in puppy classes by the majority of dog trainers in the UK. The responsible caregiver provides their puppy with what he needs nutritionally, and exposes him to the things he needs to get used to – and, hopefully, they also teach him to be confident, curious and flexible. But we seldom if ever help our puppies learn to be calm! At seven weeks and onwards through puppyhood, when a young dog is learning who he or she is and how to thrive in the domestic world, our emphasis tends to be on the active commands. We teach a sit as soon as we possibly can. We teach a down next. Then caregivers of new puppies like to teach the fun stuff: paw, fetch, bark. But we seldom bother with stay until the dog is a bit older. We don't even think to teach a relaxed settle, or to emphasise duration, we forget to reward a resting puppy or a puppy who is chewing the right thing. Caregivers are fantastic at creating that 'Uh-ho' circus when things go wrong, but we are terrible at teaching a young, quick-to-learn puppy who it is we want him to be.

For some dogs the simple trauma of being kept in kennels can cause anxiety-based behaviour problems.

RESCUED DOGS

Good people will put kindness above making the best choice, and we now live in a culture of rescued dogs. These unwanted, abandoned and stray dogs more often achieve family-owed status much later on in life than the puppies we buy from breeders. A more recent fad is adopting puppies from foreign countries. Helping dogs from around the world is generous and kind, but not enough work is done to recognise and help these dogs integrate into a whole new culture, environment and temperature!

Some of these rescued dogs come from extremely traumatic backgrounds. One of my own dogs had his ears chopped off, and I have a client dog who suffered a 'home castration'. When working at a London animal hospital I met puppies born in bins, dogs scalded with acid and even dogs stabbed and shot.

All these traumas (minor and major) can have a significant effect on behaviour, attachment and general emotional state. These dogs often suffer with anxiety and fear-based behaviour problems. They are also not as well equipped to deal with 'normal' domestic life, having so often been untrained or trained using aversive techniques, under socialised or badly socialised during their early puppyhood.

These dogs often need far more assistance in terms of teaching and learning. Their experience also means that they find the traditional learning environment daunting and pressurising. When seeing these dogs, and working with them, it becomes apparent that creating a better environment conducive to learning is something that can help all dogs and people – irrespective of background.

UNWANTED YET DESIRABLE BREED TRAITS

Different dogs were selectively bred for different reasons. Sighthounds to see, air scent and chase small furry animals; bull terriers to bait bulls and bears; gundogs to use their noses to find prey, point it out to their masters, chase it and/or to retrieve it, and herding dogs whose focus is on rounding up livestock. Many of these breed traits are redundant in a domestic setting, yet strangely desirable to many caregivers. We love it when a Vizsla points and stalks the seagulls (apart from when he won't come back, or retrieves a pet duck). Often these dogs, who are bred to be *fit for purpose* are not given any real opportunity to exhibit their natural behaviours and practise that purpose. Much of the time this builds frustration and means the dog has certain levels and types of energy which come out in unwanted behaviour.

THE DESIRE FOR CALM

All owners of domestic house dogs seem to have one desire in common, irrespective of their choice of breed or the age or background of their dogs. We want our dogs to be calm.

Calm is an adjective which means not showing or feeling nervousness, anger, or other strong emotions. Of course, we cannot train our dogs not to feel emotion. What we can do, however, is train posture, expression and action that is conducive to bringing about a calm disposition and a focused, self-controlled and positive state. We can then work on human connection and increasing posture duration to promote good mental and physical health as well as emotional strength and calmness.

In the wild (aka: in villages in places such as India where canines still roam free) dogs negotiate space and pace using postures, actions and expressions. This is natural behaviour which has functional reward (e.g. basic survival). In a domestic setting, dogs often have no control over their space. Negotiation techniques, which dogs have evolved to use successfully to adapt to life as a tame species, go unnoticed and even punished. A village dog, for example, may show a side glance, turn his head and sniff away from a threat to gain more space, and to communicate that he does not want conflict. In a domestic setting, and with a dog in a confined space or on a lead, these signals cannot be used. So when there is a perceived threat, our dogs have no option but to use stronger signals (for example, warning growls and lips curls) to gain the same effect. This stress caused by our human inability to recognise, let alone reward, good social signaling, is the seed of much frustration and stress, and results in so many of the behavioural problems that we see in domestic dogs. As I said before: dogs cannot talk but they are speaking to us all the time. We just need to learn to listen!

I have used posture training with many dogs and I feel it is a broad programme that helps in the vast majority of problem dog cases, including fear-based and frustration behaviours towards objects, dogs and people and predatory chase problems. It helps sound dogs to improve general control, dog-owner connection and general calmness, as well as enhancing our dogs' sense of wellbeing. It can also be highly successful in preventing kennel stress in rescue organisations, as well as benefiting elderly, injured or post operative dogs. Most importantly, though, it teaches us to recognise, highlight and reward more subtle communication techniques from our dogs and form a dialogue that empowers them and provides options which result in better choices.

INCREASING THE FREQUENCY OF NEGOTIATION, CALM AND SOFT BEHAVIOURS

Any behaviour that is reinforced increases in frequency. Reinforcement is, by definition, anything that strengthens or increases the frequency of a behaviour. If I give you cash every time you get me a coffee, you will get me more coffee. If we practise this 'training' frequently, other things will happen too. You will feel better, excited even, about getting me a coffee. In practising your coffee-making skills, you will get better and quicker at making my coffee, so you will be more likely to make it again in the future. You may even develop rituals around this – using your own thirst for tea, for example, as a reminder to get me a coffee and earn some cash.

If I were to reduce the money, or even start saying thanks instead of giving you any money, the rituals, habits and feel-good factor surrounding the coffee-making process would remain. You would make more coffee for me than prior to the training – and if every month or so I slipped you bonus cash for a cuppa, it might even increase the coffee making even further!

This is what happens when we reward wanted (and unwanted) behaviours with dogs. I always suggest to caregivers of breeds such as Mastiffs, not to train 'give me a paw', or Yorkie people not to train 'speak'. Don't actively reinforce stuff that you don't want to increase in frequency! Breeds have predispositions for certain traits and postures; reinforcing them just makes the dogs even more likely to practice them in their daily life! This is fine if we are teaching a sofa surfing Lurcher to settle on a sofa, but begins to cause problems if we are rewarding a naturally vocal breed for barking.

There are behaviours – posture, actions and expression – that dogs practise and, most often, we ignore. These communication strategies are very important when a dog is communicating to another dog or another species. If we were stripped of our ability to negotiate, or appease people, conflict, aggression, and feelings of powerlessness, frustration and anxiety would certainly increase. Social signalling is a way of communicating, passively, a desire or emotional state. Being able to read and adjust to these desires and emotional states when our dogs communicate them, prevents frustration and fear.

Calmness is the one trait that all caregivers want to see in their domestic house guests.

This book paves the way towards training a system of rewarding passive, socially appropriate, social signalling. In some respects we are acting as a parent would: rewarding a child for smiling with a smile in return, or rewarding them for telling us they are scared, by offering support. This dialogue is perfectly possible with our canine companions, too! And training our dogs Real Dog Yoga trains us, and them, to think differently and, hopefully, to establish a meaningful dog-human dialogue.

HOW LONG DOES IT TAKE TO TRAIN A DOG?

There is one concept that I have found really useful in life, and certainly when training dogs. It is the concept of life-long learning, which comes from the acceptance that there is no destination in dog training (or life). Death is the only ending. With this in mind, train your dogs slowly and well, and enjoy the process of learning.

There are dogs that cope well and manage successfully in their environment – and there are dogs that don't. There are dogs that follow instructions quickly and know many different commands – and others that chew shoes and spend their days frustrated and confused.

As a professional dog behaviourist, I have met dogs that will herd sheep, dogs that will scent discriminate between high and low concentration Birch, dogs that will perform the most accomplished tricks, and dogs that will dance on stage. I have also met dogs that bite people, dogs that bite dogs, dogs that chase cows, sheep, squirrels and bikes, and dogs that cannot be left without sheer panic setting in. I have never met an owner who says that their dog is trained.

The journey is never over, which is why, with patience and understanding, we should enjoy the life-long process of co-learning with our dogs.

Advice about training flows from every orifice of the Internet with extremists in each camp. The only advice I can give to those trying to navigate their way through reams of conflicting advice is that, if it feels wrong it usually is. If you feel like you are doing something that is confusing or feels bad for your dog – it isn't the right direction. If it doesn't make logical sense, find a technique that does. I meet owners who have tried every different form of 'training' from the extremely invasive – electrocuting a dog with an ecollar, or rolling him on his back and pinning him on the floor – to the totally passive. That is not touching the dog unless he asks, chastising themselves if they raise the pitch of their voice or use a word that may be interpreted as a reprimand. In this book I will recommend the methods I feel are the most humane, most appropriate for our canine companions, and most successful in teaching them the postures, expressions and actions needed to practise Real Dog Yoga.

Rewarding calm postures – and calm, soft expressions – will increase the natural occurrence of these behaviours.

18

Good teaching involves creating a good environment for the individual's learning and then clearly marking and rewarding desirable behaviour. It involves learning what makes the learner tick and how we can motivate him to choose to participate. It is about setting clear, achievable goals and, ultimately giving the learner as much of a voice as is possible in his lessons.

To successfully live with another species it is imperative we establish a dialogue. If we invite a foreign person who speaks a different verbal language, into our home, we would not dream of shouting at them if they used a word we didn't understand. We would slow what we were saying and use the words they did know to teach them the words they didn't. If we are super keen to establish a common dialogue, we might even learn some of our foreign houseguest's language, too. Establishing a common dialogue with our canines is the same. If we want to live happily together and to communicate to and fro fluently, we need to work out a way in which we can successfully communicate how we feel, and what we want, as well as understand how the individual dog feels and what he wants. Dialogue isn't: 'I say and you do'; that is command. Dialogue is about two beings being able to share information. The most important information our dogs can share with us is their emotional state because this is what drives behaviour.

Yoga is defined as the steady control of the senses. The following is a step-by-step guide to teaching your dog the postures, expressions and actions used in Real Dog Yoga, as well as an explanation of how I have used these to combat problems rooted in stress, anxiety and frustration. Follow the guide slowly and wisely. Enjoy the journey...

There is no such thing as a 'trained' dog.

Section One
AN ENVIRONMENT FOR LEARNING

The training within this book should be followed carefully. Do not jump a stage or rush a stage. Do not progress faster if you think your dog is smart. This is about taking you and your dog together on a journey of physical, mental and emotional discovery.

This is about being connected, learning patience, forgiveness and control. This is not about a destination: there is no destination. You and your dog can continue to progress and enhance your physical, mental and spiritual connection and wellbeing through gentle, organic, space filled practice – not by rushing.

Processing is one of the most important parts of the learning process, and it happens when we stop. It happens when our dogs stop, too; stopping to think rather than to do nothing. In this sense doing what looks like nothing, and what is often misperceived as disengagement, is actually a fundamental step of learning. Appropriately ascertaining what is processing behaviour, what is boredom or displacement and what is disengagement, is paramount to becoming an effective learning facilitator. This is why slowing everything down and not being afraid to break is something I will constantly

reiterate during the course of this book. The art of doing (what looks like) nothing can make the difference between a dog learning and a dog not learning.

Note: The final section of this book is about application. An important part of this training is to recognise why we are reinforcing postures, expressions and actions. Under no circumstances should we ever ask our dogs to use a posture, expression or action unnaturally in a social context. What that means is that this training is powerful stuff, and we are reinforcing behaviours we want to increase naturally. We are not doing this so that we can ask our dogs to smile when they feel sad, or to act relaxed when they feel under threat. We are training these behaviours in a controlled context where a dog is free from stressors and has exits points and space. We can mark and reward these behaviours as we

The ideal space needs to be clear, with options for the dog to leave, and water available for you both.

recognise them in natural social settings, and we can give them a meaning by giving them a function. For example, we can reinforce a natural soft eye with physical affection (showing that we recognise the expression and that this expression has meaning and serves a purpose), or we can reinforce passive stress and space negotiation signals by ensuring we increase the space between our dog and his perceived threat. This is a dialogue. This connects you and your dog and shows our canine friends that, in this human world, they still have power and control. It teaches a dog to come to us for help and that we will protect him. These things will encourage a dog to understand that he doesn't need to use aggression or conflict and that being relaxed, calm and soft is reinforcing.

HOW SHOULD EACH DOG YOGA SESSION LOOK?

- Create a clean, clear and comfortable environment for you and your dog's session.
- Count out the treats you will need to teach the posture, action or expression you are working with, and make sure you both have plenty of water available.
- Begin by taking your dog for a walk outside your home.
- Take your dog into the Yoga space and remove his collar or any other equipment.
- Train one posture, action or expression (follow the order as set out in Section Two).
- Warm your dog down mentally after each session by taking him for a game or for a cuddle afterwards.
- Ensure there is enough time to do all this. Dog Yoga sessions take around 30 minutes a day, which includes the warm up walk, the session and the warm down game or cuddle.

IF WE EXPECT ACCURACY, WE MUST PROVIDE CLARITY IN TRAINING

What is meant by clarity in training? In Dog Yoga clarity refers to providing a dog with a space which is clean from environmental, emotional and social stressors in which to train. For different dogs that means different things. I have one dog who finds magnets on the fridge extremely distracting (I once used them to practice target colour discrimination and he became fixated on nosing them all). For this dog (Archie the Pit Bull), his physical environment is extremely stimulating. To get the best out of him I must use a totally clean space.

For another dog who is a rescue (Bubbles, the Spaniel), I must ensure that I am totally 100 per cent neutral. She finds any emotional tension extremely stressful. I must be sitting down, calm and not excited, as well as very sure about what we are training. She couldn't care less if I have things on the table or a broom by the door, but just a minor emotional hint from me that there is any tension and she becomes nervous, barks and cannot learn. Learn your dog off by heart. If your dog finds something in the environment stressful, remove it.

Trainers are the same. I am someone who trains better in a clear space, but I can train irrespective of what other stressors may have occurred in my day. I have colleagues who can train their dogs in the messiest of rooms, but cannot deal with training a new behaviour until they have totally wound down from a stressful day.

We, all of us, dogs and people, learn best without distraction. I am aiming to make these sessions the best, most productive, progressive and enriching training for you and your dog. This is why you should follow the guidance and give you and your dog the best Yoga space to train – but essentially you need to discover what mess is, for you and for your dog.

CREATING AN IDEAL PHYSICAL SPACE TO TEACH DOG YOGA

The Yoga space should be warm (normal room temperature). Freezing or very hot conditions should be avoided but it is fine – so long as the weather is ok – to teach outside in the garden if you don't have enough space in the house. If you have no garden or room in the house, you can teach in a public space. To do this I suggest that you have your dog on a long line, clipped around your waist, and that you create a physical boundary so that you can mark when your dog has opted away and out of the space for a break.

We rarely think about the physical space between us and the dogs we train – but it is of the utmost importance.

If you are indoors, the floor should not be a strange texture and should ideally be natural, such as wood or carpet. This is because dogs are more comfortable and less likely to slip on this kind of flooring. A mat can be used if you don't have such flooring in your home.

A Dog Yoga mat should be a mat which is only used for this training on the floor in a space which is comfortable to the dog. Some dogs find that having a mat on the floor is difficult to accept. For example, when working with Bully breeds I have found foam mats (camping rolls), stuck to the floor work best. It is important that the mat does not become a distraction but, equally, normal dog beds are not practical to use in this sort of training context. Additionally, studies have shown us that dogs find discriminatory objects useful predictors of context. By that, I mean that if you put a red ribbon on the door every time you go out, your dog will find it easier to know what to expect from the situation. Predictable objects which can signpost our expectations are great in helping the learning environment make sense to the learner.

There should be natural light allowed in through windows and doors, so curtains should remain open. Door glass where the dog can see out should remain uncovered, too. The outside world is very rarely a distraction to a dog when he is really training. What is more commonly the case is that the dog is either using the environment as a purposeful distraction to defuse perceived tension, or that he is bored or maybe in need of time and space to process information! In any of these situations, simply covering up the outside world will not help to improve your dog's focus.

Access to another area in the house/building, or outdoors, should be available if possible. If this is not possible (for example in a shelter or veterinary consulting room) then keep a crate available and covered. Also in group training situations, pinpoint markers where, if the dog crosses the room, the owner breaks their session. For example, if a dog walks towards the door and orientates out of your field of vision, he is opting out of training.

FIXING THE ENVIRONMENT

A session should start with fixing the environment so that it is clean, clear and comfortable. Once the environment is clear, it is time to ensure we are clear too.

- There should always be access to clean, cold water for both you and your dog.

- Wash the floor before you train. This might mean sweeping, Hoovering or washing. Use pet friendly cleaner, or even just with water, and ensure the surface is dry. A clean environment makes a difference to our thinking mind and to a dog's scent orientated mind, too.

Your own posture should be comfortable regardless of whether you are sitting, crouching or standing.

TWO POTS ARE BETTER THAN ONE

Always have two pots (plates or bowls) ready for treats. One will be an active pot which is where you can count out small numbers of treats to train specific steps. This helps with clarity for the human.

The treats that are not being used for these specific steps stay in the non-active pot and the treats you are training with go in the active pot. This makes it so much easier when you are training as it negates the need to count how many repetitions you are doing, and it gives you a strategic place to stop and think through what your next step is going to be.

• Don't train where there is clutter. If your house is cluttered, choose a room, or even part of a room, and totally declutter it.

• Look through what you are training before you train it. Always. Every time.

• Ensure that you are in a good, positive and calm state of mind and then count out the treats ready for your session into a pot or plate. Then prepare 20 extra treats for the first few sessions just in case. Place the container somewhere your dog cannot access it.

A good learning facilitator manipulates the environment to make learning as easy and as enjoyable as possible. Presenting a dog with a clean, clear and comfortable environment is beneficial to a dog's learning capacity as well as our own. Dog training is a journey you take together. You both change, grow and progress together. You are both the learner and the teacher, but only you have opposable thumbs

to clean up the environment – so make sure you do so.

GETTING YOURSELF READY

Get everything ready before you bring your dog in. Some people like to warm up physically as if at the gym, so try it and see if it helps. You need to be in one stable place; your thoughts need to be clear, clean, focused and controlled, your body needs to act upon well practiced and carefully decisive impulses. If you do not find yourself ready to train your dog because you are still stressing about your day at work, worrying about the children or just generally distracted, follow the steps below...

Things to do before you train to reduce tension and stress:

1. Close your eyes and take long, deep breaths for five full minutes. Put a timer on for five minutes and practise stillness for this whole time. As the sessions progress, you

will find it takes far less time to clear your mind but for the time being start with five full minutes. It will feel like ages but trust me! Do not get up or move for this time. Try not to fidget. If you need to then put your hands somewhere specific, such as on a table, and focus on stillness. Try not to think of anything other than your breathing.

2. Drink a full pint of cold water

3. Write a down what you hope to achieve in your training session with your dog, or at least think through what you are hoping to train. This might be as simple as: "I want Marley to sit still for one minute". Try to ensure your goals are measurable, i.e. that you want your dog to do X for a specific amount of time, for a specific number of times, or on cue while you do something specific (such as leave the room).

4. Bounce a ball and click with your clicker every third, then second, then first bounce. Repeat until you are 100 per cent accurate.

Seldom is our own posture considered in dog training manuals but it is, in fact a very important thing to consider. When you are training your dog it is important that you are comfortable and able to be still. Sitting in a chair is fine but do ensure you are sitting straight and not hunched. Too many keen trainers get back problems from spending hours leaning over!

If you are training a very small or very young dog then sitting on the floor is perfectly acceptable, too. Many owners and handlers opt for standing when training dogs which isn't always the best position, especially when using the clicker, as it seems to lead us to moving our limbs around more which can be confusing for a dog. Dogs need balance and clarity which means we also need to be balanced and clear. Make sure you are an appropriate distance from your dog. You do not need to be right up close, as in this type of training, we don't touch our dogs (apart from the odd cuddle to say thanks). This distance helps a dog to learn more independently and, practically speaking, gives us more space to think. Stand or sit as close to your dog as you think, then take a step or move the chair back another step – and train from here. This is your training situ. If in doubt, try moving away until your dog moves towards you.

GETTING YOUR DOG READY

Dogs cannot learn when they are distracted or when they are uncomfortable. Before you bring your dog into your Yoga space, take him outside for five minutes on a lead. Practise loose lead walking. Dogs have a jogging pace and an amble pace and, generally speaking, a 'normal' human pace causes a dog to stride in-between their natural gait. This is uncomfortable and not balanced, so try to speed up or slow down to match your dog. Wander round the garden slowly, or quickly, at your dog's natural pace. Give him the opportunity to sniff and take in the air for five minutes. Let him go to the loo and have a drink if he wants one. Return to the Yoga space; unclip the lead, remove the collar or harness and see if your dog is happy to follow you and seems attentive to go into training.

Taking off your dog's collar, and any other equipment he wears, ensures he is comfortable. It also means we can see his body more clearly and he can use it more freely.

We never train more than one new Real Dog Yoga posture, action or expression at a time because, when in training, we want extreme clarity. We are teaching a dog to move slowly and to be aware of his own body in a way he has not experienced before. Even the simplest postures are hard work and require a clarity of mind from both dog and practitioner to create communication connection. It requires accuracy and good timing, which is only possible if we are extremely clear about what we want. We can create a flowing dialogue where small body motions are interpreted as meaningful by the dog. It is extraordinary to see and, emotionally, it is a very beautiful and positive thing. This is a developing cross species dialogue, albeit in early formation.

Depending on your dog's natural state, sessions may last longer or less than 30 minutes. Dogs need time to de-escalate and time to process, and so do we. The longer the session, the more breaks you and your dog need. The number of breaks should increase as the session progresses, so while the first five to ten minutes may be straight up training, the last ten minutes may have as many as three, minute-long breaks. Walk outside or follow the break protocol outlined below.

Having created an environment that is conducive to learning, and with clarity in the forefront of your mind, postures should be clear, clean and comfortable – both physically and mentally. A dog needs space: physical distance from us, space in time to process, and space from physical, mental or spiritual contexts which may bring about feelings of attachment, resentment or suffering.

The training requires processing and physical awareness on the dog's part. We are hoping to see a change of physical, emotional and spiritual state in base form. This is only possible when a pupil is truly connected to a teacher. The dialogue in this training is constant and flowing. It has no beginning and no end; it is a flow of communicative thoughts and emotions which are understood by the dog through scent, sound and movement, and by us through a new found awareness and understanding of our dog's body. This requires work from the dog and from the practitioner.

Option training is the favoured format for learning in Dog Yoga (and in my view, in any form of learning) as the process should never be forced or pressured. With clarity and a lack of pressure in mind, sessions should always be kept short and sweet. By this, I mean that they should be short, short, short...not to mention fun!

JUST PLAYING...

Play has a function. The function of play is to experiment and the consequence is to learn. We try things out in a non-pressured, free state and do things that feel right, good and interesting. We are rewarded for curiosity with learning which makes play productive – but there is no goal. Play has no end or specific goal other than the personal and flexible goals we give ourselves during the process.

The renowned psychologist, Jean Piaget looked at children as "little scientists" and Soviet psychologist Lev Vygotsky suggested that play "scaffolded" (helped along) by an another was best in terms of learning. Dogs can also be viewed as little scientists. They play with their environment and we direct their learning by giving their actions and decisions a valuable functional reward. A dog barks, we give him attention; he jumps up, we touch him.

Learning through play is both natural and extremely effective. With this in mind, Dog Yoga sessions (and any training sessions) should be designed to facilitate a playful type of learning – and there is nothing better in these sessions than seeing expressions of joy. Frustration and boredom in training must be avoided at all costs. If we are to call ourselves force-free trainers, we have to aim at training without force. That includes any form of mental force. For this reason, I don't really like the term 'teacher' or 'trainer'. We are simply facilitating learning – that is what good, force-free practitioners do.

We create an environment where learning is possible and likely, both for the dog and for us. For, in Dog Yoga, we often learn as much as our canines; it is a two-way process. We then provide direction and scaffolding while the dog plays and learns what will get him rewards. It is important that we realise that play is not the opposite of work.

It is so important to value play; it is the best, most enjoyable way to learn.

Play that is given direction and function ensures that dogs learn from their current skills and prior knowledge. This learning is independent, enjoyable and seems to be intrinsically stimulating for our canine friends.

PRINCIPLES OF LEARNING

EXPERIMENTATION

Initially, in most of the postures, expressions and actions, we actively reward our dogs for experimentation. In the first few sessions, this process will take longer. We are reinforcing creativity but until that creative thinking has become a practised way of learning, the session, to the dog it may seem just like any other play session. As the sessions progress however, the dog will learn that in every session a different posture, action or expression is reinforced. This concept learning is very important and teaches our dogs to think creatively and offer us different things.

Ella is experimenting to find out what will earn her the reward. Initially, I reward her first for simply touching the target anywhere with her nose.

After practicing with other parts of her body she realises that only nose touches are rewarding so she begins to repeat this.

When Ella understands the goal for the exercise, I reward her only when she touches the bullseye.

To help the process along, each session begins with the dog exploring. We often give him clues by asking a known position first (such as a sit or a down) but then, we can let him think. He may try a variety of different shapes and movements and as good learning facilitators we should never, ever punish this. That means while our dogs experiment we don't say "no" or "uh-uh" or give him reinforcement that he is wrong. Dog trainers call this type of verbal reinforcement 'non-reward markers'. NRMs are predictive of nothing, and I have found that natural extinction (letting the dog learn independently that practicing this incorrect posture won't get him his reward), increases creativity in future sessions. Using NRMs reduces independent learning in my view, and also reduces creativity, particularly in obedience trained and fearful dogs.

Dog Yoga is a process not a destination and so, with this in mind, all parts of the learning process are positive and progressive. Getting it wrong is simply a part of getting it right. In fact, if anything, we should encourage the offering of new behaviours with smiles and by feeling pleased that our dogs are experimenting – and certainly not be punishing it.

REPEATED PRACTICE

The second principle of learning in Dog Yoga is Repeated Practice. Repeated Practice in the sessions happens in a bell graph. This is when a dog gets on the right track, practises the reinforced behaviour a few times, then seems to 'forget' and starts trying out to see if other things can get him the reward instead. It is at this point I would usually break and then begin giving the dog a more structured hand signal or a verbal cue (more scaffolding) on his return.

FINE TUNING

The third and final learning principle is Fine Tuning. During this phase the dog has worked out what is earning him the click and treat, so this time our goal is to get stronger, longer behaviours. Our dogs are fine tuning precisely what gets them their treat, with the help of a clear environment and markers to clarify they are heading in the right direction.

EXPERIMENTATION, REPEATED PRACTICE AND FINE TUNING...

So, for example, let us look at teaching Nora, the Border Terrier, to do a left neck stretch. To begin she comes into the Yoga space and sniffs around. We ask for a "sit" and, being that this is the third session, she recognises that she can earn treats in this context if she does something. Initially, she may paw or bark or simply sit very straight. All this is good as she is experimenting. As she turns her head slightly we click and give her a treat. We are scaffolding (i.e. directing) her experimentation and giving her play-learning a direction. Nora then repeatedly practises this neck turn four times and earns four treats. She then paws again...nothing. Hmm. So she then gets up and moves around.

In exiting the Yoga space, a good facilitator recognises that Nora needs a processing break so gets up and drinks some water while the dog moves outside, has a little sniff around then returns to her facilitator's side. She repeat practises the head moves, repeating

the posture 10 times with more confidence.

The facilitator recognises that significant learning has taken place and gives the neck stretch a verbal cue and hand gesture. Nora practises five more times on the cue of her facilitator. The facilitator begins to only click and treat certain neck stretches (the longest ones) and Nora fine tunes this command until on the command "left stretch" she holds her neck up to the left until she hears the click to move her head back.

TRAINING USING TREATS

We use a clicker and treats to teach a dog the postures. This is the clearest and most effective way to teach a dog to do what we want. In time, the postures will become intrinsically meaningful and positive to your dog but, while we teach them, there are some really important things to remember about food and training.

We are using the clicker and treats as a way to show the dog that we want him to use that limb, take that posture, stay in that position for longer, etc. We are not simply teaching the dog to follow treats; we want him to enjoy the journey and to learn with us. To do this I believe that optional shaping is the most progressive way, where possible, to allow a dog to make sufficient choices for optimum learning.

Motivation is the key, but often an assumption is made that we need to use the highest motivator in dog training. In fact, using the most valued food reward for a dog is often counter productive in learning facilitation. What is important is that we choose the right motivator. The correct motivation will help the learning process and thus accelerate learning. If I try to train a Labrador with chicken, sardines, peanut butter or beef jerky, the likelihood of him being able to use his brain is negligible. Equally, if we starve him of his dinner or breakfast before we train him, we are not only causing him suffering and teaching him that life is unpredictable, we are also reducing his ability to concentrate.

1. Choose a medium value treat. For food-mad dogs this could be a bit of kibble from his everyday food. For an unmotivated sighthound, this might be a bit of smoked salmon (see the list of options below). Don't choose anything that will stop your dog from focusing on the task, but equally don't opt for something that your dog is not bothered about. You are looking for the equivalent of a packet of crisps – not a bit of broccoli, but not a Mars bar either!

2. The treats should be cut up very small. For a Jack Russell sized dog we are talking about half the size of a child's little finger nail; for a Mastiff, about half the size of a man's thumb nail.

3. The treats should be hard enough to be dropped on the floor without making a mess.

4. The treats should be solid enough for the dog to be able to swallow comfortably.

5. Ideally treats should not be too salty nor too sweet. Everything in moderation!

6. Remember you will be counting these treats into groups so try to make them easy to handle.

7. Additionally, please remember to change his food portion appropriately and count the treats as part of his food portion.

GETTING THE MOST OUT OF EACH TREAT

When you are training remember that it is not just the type of treat that affects the value of the reward; the way we give the dog his treat can increase or decrease motivation, too. For example, we can be very vocal – "what's this, what's this, are you ready…" etc, – let the dog have an anticipatory sniff of the food and, after the training criteria is met, we throw the treat for the dog to chase and only then let him eat it. In this instance, for many dogs, we are increasing the value of the treat significantly. If we want to increase energy, we increase motivation to earn the reward. If the dog is too fixated or becoming over-excited, try rewarding him straight from your hand into his mouth a few times. This can take the energy down a notch!

It is worth bearing in mind the amount of energy we use when rewarding a dog. I suggest we should be reinforcing a dog with the energy we want from him. If we want a still sit, we should reward calmly, ideally dropping the treat or feeding straight from an open hand into the dog's mouth. But if we want movement and more energy from the dog, we should reward with movement and energy - perhaps tossing the treat and increasing anticipatory excitement with verbal excitement.

TREATS TO TRY

An assortment of the foods listed below, all in one pot, jumbled up with a little garlic pressed in:

- **Salmon**
- **Sardine (dried)**
- **Kibble soaked in sardine oil and put in the fridge for 24 hours**
- **Cubes of cheese**
- **Ham**
- **Sausage**
- **Chicken**
- **Lamb**
- **Chopped banana**
- **Chopped carrot**
- **Chopped apple**
- **Normal dry kibble (various but ideally not too high in protein)**

PACE OF TRAINING

The pace of training refers to how quickly we change the criteria to achieve a posture, action or expression. The pace that you teach your dog a posture, action or expression depends on your dog. Try not to have pre-formed ideas about your dog based on his breed, age or background. There are Bassett Hounds who learn quicker than Collies and puppies who need more space and time to learn than elderly dogs. Each dog will have his preferred pace which depends on his learning brain, ability to understand you, satiation (when he has had enough) and enjoyment of the training.

As you work through the sessions you will begin to learn about your dog's brain and how he uses it. He may need lots of breaks but can do lots of mini sessions in a row, or he may prefer fewer breaks, longer sessions, but treats coming thick and fast.

When you start, keep the pace slow. This is the reason that you need to count out the treats for each criteria. Each treat should be considered. How quickly did your dog perform the desired behaviour? How confident was his body language? Has he 'got it'? If your dog is 'getting it' truly, then moving on quickly is the correct choice. Getting a dog to repeat and repeat the same behaviour, for the same outcome, will become frustrating or boring. However, asking him to move on to the next criteria before he has had that 'light bulb moment' is confusing and will reduce his motivation to learn. I have worked out a guide for the number of treats you will need for each criteria in Section Two, but remember that this is just approximation. The treat guides are merely an average over-view based on lots of dogs, in lots of environments. You may want to count an extra 20 treats in each pot for your dog and break criteria down into even smaller steps. You may also find that your dog may get through some steps very quickly. If your learning pace is appropriate and your frequency of reward is correct, we should not see any frustration and learning should be fast and fun!

A dog may stop and scratch as a way of defusing tension; it may also be a sign of frustration or an indication that he needs time to process.

You know you can move to the next criteria if your dog has increased the frequency and the intensity of the action you are clicking. After you have done a few sessions, you will become better at spotting those light bulb moments when your dog realises: "ah, that's what is getting the click". When this happens, it is time to move forward or start fine tuning.

FREQUENCY OF REWARD

How often you treat a dog is an extremely important consideration. It also depends on the individual dog. The golden rule is that if motivation is going down – i.e. if your dog is seemingly becoming distracted or disinterested – lower the criteria and increase the reward. What that means is that you need to make the task easier, and give him more treats for less.

For example, you are teaching Ralph to spin so may be rewarding him for moving his body in a half-circle to the left. If Ralph loses interest, you need to start rewarding the quarter-circles. This makes it easier for him as it is a task he has already accomplished. Because he finds it easier, he increases how many times he does the quarter circles and thus increases how many clicks and treats he gets. This usually increases energy and motivation so that you can then move forward in a better state of mind. However, sometimes this is can be a sign that your dog needs a little break.

Ideally, in this sort of training clicks and treats should be coming thick and fast. There is no better sound, so click and treat away!

OPTIONAL CLICKER SHAPING: WHAT DOES THIS MEAN?

TRAINING WITH OPTIONS

Option training means, simply, that the dog has lots of options during training including the option not to train. He can leave at any time and choose to participate, or not, in the learning. This empowers the dog and ensures that the decision to train is both yours and your dog's. The dog can take breaks when he chooses, just as you can. He can also decide that he doesn't want to take part. He can speed things up, or show you that he needs to slow things down. We must be in tune with our dogs to read these desires in order to get the most enjoyment out of the sessions. Once we are in tune, option training creates a powerful type of dual communicative learning which, not only enhances the bond between dog and owner but also seems to open up the dog's learning mind.

There should be exits made available for a dog to leave, unfollowed, and an owner needs to be continually aware of behaviours which may suggest their dog needs a break. We will go on to discuss this further, but when we use option training we must be mindful that the dog is always opting in to learn.

This ensures that the time we spend teaching him is as productive and positive as possible. Force-free training is not just training without smacking, shocking or pinching. True force-free training removes any notion of force – forcing a dog to train with you still counts as force – so make sure he's got the choice to take part or not.

Ella can leave the space at any time but here it is her choice to engage with me and choose to participate.

TRAINING WITH A CLICKER

A clicker is a little metal box or button that, when pressed, makes a clicking noise.

Clicker training is a method developed and popularised by Karen Pryor in the 1980s via a phenomenally popular book called *Don't Shoot The Dog*. The method was first introduced when she was working with marine mammals and then later used to teach domestic and companion animals. The method is simple, and people are often stunned by the results that are achieved simply by using a small plastic box that makes a clicking noise.

SO, HOW DOES CLICKER TRAINING WORK?

1. The learning facilitator creates an environment where a dog is likely to participate in a desirable behaviour. For example, placing a mat on the floor for a dog to sit on.

2. We mark the action – for example, the dog's bottom hitting the floor – with a "click".

Clickers comes in a variety of shapes and colours but all work on the same principle of producing a click when pressed.

3. We follow up each click with a food reward.

4. We repeat this until the dog starts repeating the behaviour more frequently with more intensity.

5. Then we remove, or begin to remove, our encouragement of the rewarded behaviour. So, in this example, we would slowly remove the mat (perhaps folding it in half, then in half again before taking it away completely).

6. We then wait for the dog to choose to repeat the behaviour. This would involve the dog choosing to sit without the mat.

7. We then mark every time the dog repeats the action with the click and a treat.

8. We reward every time we click.

9. Then we add a cue – a word and/or a gesture – to help the dog predict what we want them to do.

A dog is conditioned by the clicker. His brain pairs the noise with the treat. We then teach him that his actions can cause the noise to happen. He then begins to work for the click, knowing it always leads to a food reward. The tool can be used to mark clearly when the dog has done what we want him to do. This gives us more time to then fish a treat from the pot or treat pouch before he loses the connection of action and reward. Learning can occur without a clicker if you are simply treating a dog each time he performs the desired behaviour, but it seems to be far slower and there is much more pressure on us, the learning facilitator, to get the treats to the dog quickly – something that few people are good at.

VERBAL CUES

In this type of training we add verbal cues after a behaviour is being repeatedly practised accurately. So, if we are teaching a sit, the word to ask the dog to perform the sit should only be introduced when the dog understands what we want. We first train the dog that to earn the click and treat, they have to sit. We then begin to ask "sit" and then reward the behavior only when it is cued. The dog can accurately predict that we want that behaviour based on us making this specific noise – in this case saying the word "sit". When we introduce verbal cues they should be spoken clearly first, maybe followed by a hand signal or some form of encouragement. This is clear and doesn't confuse a dog. It teaches him that the sound "sit" is a reliable predictor that this behaviour will be reinforced.

If we start saying "sit" during the process of training and before the posture is being reliably held, it muddies the meaning of the sound. Additionally, if we ask "sit" at the same time as using a hand signal the dog already knows, he won't be listening or acting upon the word but will simply react to the hand signal. He will still learn the word but it will take longer and be less clear.

Now that Alfie is frequently looking up to gain his reward, it makes sense to give the behaviour a name which works as a verbal cue.

SHAPING

Shaping is simply one way to use the clicker. Shaping involves clicking and rewarding an approximation of the behaviour we would like to put on cue, and then changing the training criteria to increase accuracy until the dog is completing the whole desired behaviour. For some postures, expressions and actions it is harder to use shaping but we try, where we can, to use this method.

This method highly stimulates the brain. It is, in my view, the most effective form of communicative learning between owner and dog. The dog has to work out what part of his body moving causes the click. He has to offer his ideas. Whilst perhaps this is initially hard for a dog to grasp, once learning has occurred

Initially, I reward Archie for taking two feet off the floor in any way.

To get a symmetrical beg, I only reward when his legs are at the same height.

through shaping, the dog is fully participating, mentally. In terms of the development of a thinking brain, this is preferable to luring a dog into position, or capturing a behaviour when it occurs naturally with the clicker, which usually takes longer, is harder for the facilitator to control and is less conducive to establishing a positive human-dog dialogue.

For example, let us look at a simple instruction: spin left (complete a full circle left, on the spot).

If we teach our dog to spin left with a lure instead of by shaping, we will begin by taking a treat and encouraging the dog to follow the treat in a circle, clicking the mid point. We will then fade the treat lure which means slowly, over repetitions, reducing how much we use our hand to encourage the dog to circle. We then begin clicking three-quarters of a circle and then a complete circle. We reduce the hand signal until we can simply point and then click after the dog has completed the spin. Once this is being repeated accurately we start using the verbal cue as a precursor that this behaviour will the dog earn the reward.

If we capture this behaviour, we will wait for the dog to spin left by himself naturally and when we see this behaviour occur we click and treat it. We then wait until it is repeated before we click and treat the dog. Only when the dog is actively repeating the spin frequently would we bring in the verbal cue.

When shaping this behaviour, we begin by clicking any approximation of the behaviour. So, we would click and treat the dog when he looked to the left, however slight a movement this may be. We would do a few repetitions of this and then only click the most pronounced head turns. After repetitions of this we would expect to see an increase in the frequency in which the dog is offering that behaviour (i.e. we would see more head turns offered). We would also expect to see an increase in intensity (i.e. the head turns would be more confident). Once the frequency and intensity has increased we would hold off the click until the dog works out he needs to turn slightly to the left with his body to get the click. We would continue this process until the dog is turning his whole body around to get the reward. We would then bring in the verbal cue.

Shaping uses natural 'extinction bursts' to give the learning facilitator an opportunity to mark and reward a higher intensity behaviour, and then to fine tune it. What does that mean? An extinction burst is an increase in the intensity and/or frequency of a behaviour when something that used to have a certain consequence, suddenly doesn't. The best

analogy of this comes from Karen Pryor's book *Don't Shoot The Dog*. She says that it is like putting 50 pence into a vending machine and not getting your can of drink. What do you do? You would probably hit the chosen drink's button harder (increase the intensity of the behaviour which, historically, earned you the can of drink), and repeatedly (increase the frequency of the behaviour which, historically, earned you the drink). You would maybe put in another 50p in. This is an extinction burst. In shaping, when we hold off from using the clicker, we are making use of this little burst of behaviour and using it to get a more intense result. Obviously when we are doing this it is very important to be aware of frustration. It is a very fine line we are walking, so making sure your slight criteria change doesn't stress the dog is paramount to the sessions staying fun, and the dog continuing to opt in. This is shaping.

SHAPING OUT

When training Dog Yoga we only work on one thing at a time. So, for example, if your dog is raising a particular paw higher while you are teaching a beg, you would continue clicking the desirable behaviour (two paws off the ground) and ignore the undesirable one (one paw being raised higher). After the desirable behaviour is on cue (i.e. you can ask for "beg" and your dog brings both front paws off the ground), you can then begin shaping out the undesirable behaviour that has accompanied it. In this example, it would mean that we would only click when the paw raising is a little more symmetrical. Then we raise our criteria further and refine the posture by only clicking when both paws are exactly the same height. This is just a part of fine tuning.

Dogs need to be given the time and space to run off the intensity of the sessions and process what they are learning.

BREAK PROTOCOLS

There are many reasons why a break may be necessary both for you and for your dog. Generally, not enough breaks are taken in training and, I would suggest you probably need to double the number of breaks you are taking when training your dog in any area to increase his performance. It is not just a dog that needs breaks to process information constructively; you may also need to opt out if training is not happening as you would like. Equally, your dog may want to opt out if he isn't feeling great, something more exciting is going on elsewhere, or if he just isn't ready to move forward. All these reasons are good reasons to break.

I have included break points in nearly all of the posture, actions and expression guides, but you can break whenever you or your dog feels like it.

Processing forms a very important part in the learning process which is why it is so vital for us, and our canine companions to take breaks. When you take a break, follow the steps below:

1. Walk out of the Yoga space.

2. Drink some water and offer your dog water, too.

3. Focus on what you hoped to achieve and what action point you were clicking, or will be clicking next, while your dog wanders, ideally outdoors with an opportunity to empty his bladder.

4. Take a deep breath and evaluate your
mental state:

- Do you feel clear about exactly what you
are training?
- Do you feel patient?
- Do you feel positive, relaxed and
connected to your dog?

If you can confidently say yes to all three
criteria, re-enter the space and wait for your
dog to join you. You can call him but if he
chooses to exit again, step away from the
clicker and sit on the floor with your dog.
Today's training is cancelled; today you can
have cuddles or a game instead.

Remember how important forgiveness
and love is in a relationship, and also
remember that your dog doesn't have any
specific destination in mind, and nor should
you. Training is only fun, progressive and
positive if you are both complicit in the
process. In the long run, more learning
occurs if you work to this pattern, and it
also increases the motivation to enter the
sessions.

If, during a session, your dog decides to
exit where a break has not been scheduled,
let him. Do not call him back. Wait for
him to opt back in. You should take this
opportunity to take a break, too and try
again in a moment. Time should not be an
emotional or thought-worthy constraint in
this type of dog training – only a physical
one. So if you worry that waiting for your
dog is taking up precious time, call it a day
on the training and continue tomorrow or
next time you are free.

BUILDING DURATION WITH A CLICKER

With all of the postures we are looking for
stillness. That means we, ideally, want our
dogs to hold the postures. To do this we teach
the dog that the clicker releases them from
what they are being asked to do. In Section
Two of the book we go into detail as to how
to teach this duration with the first posture
("Sit") but the method is the same for all the
postures.

We teach a dog that the clicker signals the
end of what they are being asked to do. To do
this we ask the dog to go into the posture (e.g.
down). We then reward the dog directly with a
treat whilst he is in the posture but without a
click. If he breaks the position, we simply ask
the dog to reproduce the posture. Then treat to
the mouth, take a step away, take a step back,
treat to the mouth again, then click and treat
on the ground in front of the dog to prompt
him to exit the posture.

If we are asking for a movement like a spin, we
ask the dog to spin, reward to the mouth, then
wait (without asking) for another spin, reward
to the mouth then click and treat the dog by
tossing a treat on the floor. We then wait for
two spins (spin-pause-spin) before rewarding
– but not clicking – and repeat, mixing up how
many spins the dog must produce to earn the
treat. We are teaching the dog to continually
repeat the action until he hears the click.

We then build on this. For example, we ask
the dog to go into a lie flat position. We wait,
and reward directly to his mouth. We then
take a step away, and step back. If the dog

39

Lily learns that it pays to stay where she is. Slowly I can ask for a longer and longer stand.

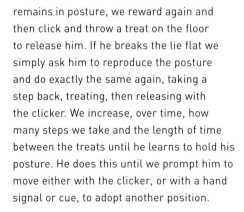

remains in posture, we reward again and then click and throw a treat on the floor to release him. If he breaks the lie flat we simply ask him to reproduce the posture and do exactly the same again, taking a step back, treating, then releasing with the clicker. We increase, over time, how many steps we take and the length of time between the treats until he learns to hold his posture. He does this until we prompt him to move either with the clicker, or with a hand signal or cue, to adopt another position.

This teaches your dog that it pays to stay. It builds the control and teaches the dog that when he is asked to go into one posture, he has to hold the position and practise stillness, impulse and muscle control until told otherwise. When we chain behaviours together we mix this up a little bit. It may seem that this

contradicts the pays to stay training. It doesn't – but we will go into this later!

FRUSTRATION OR BOREDOM IN A SESSION

Scratching, rolling, playing, barking, mouthing or whining in a session is usually a sign of frustration or confusion. When a dog is repeatedly asked to achieve something and he doesn't fully understand what is wanted, it can cause intense frustration. Equally, when a dog learns something and is asked to repeat it over and over, again with the same consequence, it can become boring. Scratching, rolling, playing, barking, mouthing or whining are generally signs of boredom or frustration which is not at all what this training (or any form of training) should be about.

It is important to recognise signs of frustration or boredom and to adjust training accordingly.

There are a few different things to try if you begin to see frustration or boredom behaviours occurring in your sessions. But, essentially you should probably take a break and think about your pace, frequency of reward and how appropriate your criteria is. If you are still seeing these behaviours occur and feel stuck, try the following:

Lower your criteria and increase your reward: Make it really easy for your dog by breaking the behaviour down further into more achievable steps. That means, if you are trying to teach him to raise his paw, start just clicking any paw movement and then begin the shaping process from here. This will regain his attention and should make the session more interesting again.

Practise a few repetitions of things he already knows: All dogs have default positions they find easy. These are usually "sit" "down" "touch" "give-me-your-paw" – that kind of thing. If your dog begins to feel frustrated or bored, ask him to do a few repetitions of things he knows well, and enjoys doing, then resume training but go back a step from where you left off.

Take a break: Everyone needs time and space to process new information. This will also prevent your getting frustrated or resentful. Go and have a glass of water, read through the exercise again and encourage your dog to let off steam outside before inviting him back, or waiting for him to re-enter the Yoga space.

Call it a day just for today: Dogs have bad days just the same as we do! If your dog is having one of those days where he is not enjoying the training, take him for a walk instead and try again tomorrow.

SECTION TWO
HOW TO TRAIN
REAL DOG YOGA

POSTURES

There are 30 postures in Dog Yoga and they fall into three sets: sit, stand and down. Each posture teaches your dog to control muscles and to control and use his body consciously.

This can help him to become less impulsive. Dogs are often driven almost entirely by impulse. Many of the problems we have in day-to-day life with our domestic dogs are caused by a lack of impulse control. Teaching a dog how to use his body also improves health and agility.

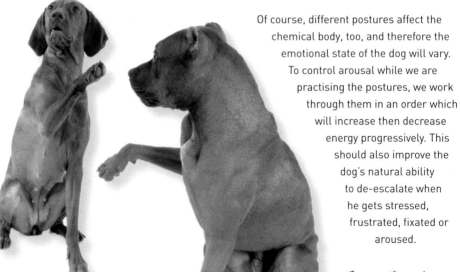

Of course, different postures affect the chemical body, too, and therefore the emotional state of the dog will vary. To control arousal while we are practising the postures, we work through them in an order which will increase then decrease energy progressively. This should also improve the dog's natural ability to de-escalate when he gets stressed, frustrated, fixated or aroused.

If you have multiple dogs, you can practise postures together. This can help dogs to focus around distractions.

Additionally, many postures are based on natural canine body language, most specifically postures which are used to negotiate and to express a desire for a non-confrontational situation. The best human way to explain why this is so useful is to relate it to smile therapy for adults. By practising positions which lead to desirable consequences we are helping the dog to learn and practise these postures which, in turn, leads to an increase in the frequency that he chooses to use them in natural behaviour. This is much the same as why smile therapy makes people happier in their natural life.

ACTIONS

There are 15 actions in Real Dog Yoga. They differ from the postures in that they are not held; they are based on very slow, careful motions. The actions look to mimic actions used to negotiate, defuse and communicate effectively during social situations.

They are put on cue to increase the frequency in which they are displayed naturally and help dogs to learn to self soothe, regain calmness and increase flexibilty, muscle control and body consciousness.

EXPRESSIONS

The 10 expressions are taught in a way which is slightly more complex than the postures and actions. This is simply because dogs express more naturally and it is much harder to gain conscious control of these movements. In my experience, a dog appears less conscious about how to use the muscles in his face and on his head. Therefore, capturing and context prompting (i.e. changing the environment to make an expression more likely to occur naturally) is used to train the expressions. They are the last thing you teach your dog in basic Dog Yoga as they are the most complicated to teach.

By putting actions such as a shake-off on cue, you will become more observant and more responsive to what your dog is saying.

A good understanding, awareness and connection, built up through teaching the postures and actions, is needed first.

Before every session ask yourself...
* Am I emotionally open and clear?
* Am I focused and clear about what I am training?
• Have I read through the exercise twice?
* Do I feel physically agile, quick with my clicker and confident?
* Have I bounced a ball and clicked the first bounce, then the second then the third with accuracy?
Yes to all the above?

Expressions should be left until last when the learning facilitator has gained a good understanding of their dog and of the clicker.

* Is my space clear?
* Is my space freshly cleaned?
* Is the space comfortable for my dog?
* Is there clean water for me and for my dog?
Yes to the above?

* Do I have enough treats?
* Have I counted the treats out ready for my exercise?
* Are the other treats in a safe, concealed, non-distracting or available place?
* Is my clicker comfortable in my hand?
Yes to the above?

* Have I taken my dog out for five minutes first?
* Has he had an opportunity to go to the loo?
* Has he been offered water?
* Does he seem calm?
* Does he seem clear?
* Does he seem happy?
* Does he seem comfortable?
* Have I removed his collar as well as anything else he wears?
Yes to the above?

* Now offer your dog a free treat.
* Now open the door so that he has the option at all times to leave...

You are ready to begin training today's posture/movement or expression:

SESSION 1
SIT

SESSION 1:1 SIT ("SIT")

The sit posture is a natural position for most, but not all dogs. Many Lurchers, Salukis and Greyhounds find getting into a sitting posture difficult and uncomfortable. With these breeds, the whole sit sequence should be skipped. Dog Yoga is about a relaxed, positive type of control; it is not about asking a dog to get into postures he may find awkward. Dog Yoga is force-free in every respect. To understand and accept what force means for your dog, you need to appreciate who your dog is, his limitations, things he finds hard and things he is good at.

Ideally, the sit we are looking for has a symmetrical upper body and a relaxed lower body. Some dogs, and dogs with weak hips, often prefer to sit to one side. This is perfectly acceptable in the Dog Yoga sit pose. We are not looking for a standard obedience sit; emphasis should be put on maintaining a relaxed disposition with calm focus and

soft eyes. The sit is the base for the rest of this sequence. You cannot rush this. It is quite usual for an owner committed to de-escalating and calming a dog, to spend a week or so practicing long, relaxed sits with duration. The dog should enjoy the sit and find it rewarding, which means we must make it rewarding.

What you will need:
• Clicker
• 35 treats
• Yoga space
• A pot with your treats (non-active), and an empty second pot to count the treats for each step into before you use them (active).

We will lure the sit as opposed to shaping it. The command is basic, commonsense and easier to teach in this way.

The sit.

45

1. Count out ten treats into your active pot.
2. Hold a treat in one hand and your clicker in the other.
3. Allow your dog to smell the treat in the hand (mmm...yummy!).
4. Hold the treat just above your dog's head so that he reaches up and lowers his rear end down to get to it.
5. Click with your clicker as soon as your dog's bottom hits the floor.
6. Treat your dog by tossing the treat on the floor so he has to get up to find it and eat it. If your dog nearly sits but not quite, you can still click and treat this behaviour a couple of times before you wait for the full sit and then click. In this way, you are making it very clear to him what you desire.
7. Repeat this until you have used up your ten treats.
8. Count 15 treats and put them into your active pot.
9. Now wait and hold your hand in a fist with a treat up and out in front of your body.
10. Be patient and practise slow breathing.
11. As soon as your dog's bottom hits the floor, click and throw a treat a little way in front of him so that he has to move to get it.
12. Repeat this 15 times.
13. Take a break and remember to follow the break protocol, encouraging your dog to stretch his legs and empty.
14. Now return to the Yoga space and get the remaining treats ready, with one in your hand.
15. First say "sit" and then hold your fist out in front of your body.
16. Wait for your dog's bottom to hit the floor.
17. Click and treat.
18. Repeat until you have used the remaining ten treats.

End your session and reward your dog at the end with a handful of treats and scatter it across the lawn for him to find.

SESSION 1:2

For this next session repeat your sit practice and build on duration

You will need:
• Clicker
• 30 treats
• An active pot and a passive pot
• Yoga space

1. Count out ten treats.
2. Ask your dog to "sit".
3. Withhold the click when the dog's bottom touches the floor this time, and take a step away from him and then towards him.
4. Treat him directly to his mouth but do not click.
5. Click and toss a treat on the floor.
6. Repeat again but walk two steps away, then three, then four, then five.
7. Click and throw the last treat on the floor, and say "ok" to release your dog.
8. Count out ten more treats.
9. Ask your dog to "sit", and withhold the click when the dog's bottom touches the floor.
10. Take multiple steps away and turn away from your dog, too.
11. Return and treat him directly to his mouth – your dog is learning that it pays to stay.
12. Repeat this, walking all around the room and treating your dog sporadically until there is only one treat left in the active pot.
13. Say "ok", click and throw the treat on the floor to release your dog.
14. Take a break.

15. Count out the remaining ten treats.
16. Ask your dog to "sit".
17. Now walk out of the room, then return to treat your dog.
18. Repeat this until there is only one treat left. Say "ok", click and throw that treat on the floor to release your dog.

The duration sit.

Build this up until you are walking round and round your dog, rewarding every now and then. Once your dog is capable of holding the sit while you move around the room, you can then move on to the stretch-left. We want the dog to enjoy the session so make sure you reward frequently. Paying him to remain in his posture is worthwhile.

The release cue is the clicker and the word "ok". So, give him the verbal cue "ok", click to release your dog out of the sit and then throw a treat on the floor to prompt the release.

If your dog gets up during a duration sit, simply lure him back to the place in the space where he began, ask him to "sit" and try again. This time perhaps take fewer steps away from him, or treat him more quickly and work up the duration more slowly.

NECK STRETCHES AND HEAD TILTS

In canine body language a 'look away' (head turn away from centre) is considered to be an appeasement gesture. When it is combined with happy, soft eyes, which look in the same direction as the nose is facing, this signal indicates to others that they may negotiate closer into that dog's space. When combined with eyes that show the white, and tense language, then the look away shows that the dog is stressed and that he would rather avoid conflict. In both contexts the dog is avoiding conflict, negotiating space and suggesting that he is not a threat.

A good example is a dog who is frightened of other dogs. When sighting another dog he may look, and then turn his head away. The other dog may mirror this behaviour on approach, and the dogs may avoid each other and arc past rather than meet. They have a mutual understanding that they would both like to appease one another rather than engage in conflict.

The head coming down, as if in a sniff, is also used in a lot of social situations. A passive sniff can be used to negotiate space from or towards another dog, or simply as displacement behaviour when a dog is trying to become invisible in order to avoid stress and potential conflict. Of course, actual sniffing is a sign of a relaxed, happy, busy dog.

Anyone who practises active dog sports such as agility or flyball will agree that stretching is very important. The conventional way to get a dog to stretch is the 'follow the treat' technique. Dogs are held between the handler's legs and lured to look left and right with a treat. However, this does not help the dog to fully stretch his muscles and, often, over-focus on the treat stops proper stretching from occurring. It can also result in over stretching as treat-keen dogs will over stretch to reach the reward.

For Dog Yoga we teach neck stretches on cue. This enhances core muscle strength and flexibility and improves control and body consciousness.
Any behaviour that is reinforced in training increases in natural behaviour. By reinforcing passive signals, like the look away as well

as other postures and expressions, we are increasingly the likelihood of our dogs practising passive appeasement rather than conflict in the future.

SESSION 1:3: SIT LEFT NECK STRETCH ("STRETCH LEFT")

What you will need:
• Clicker
• 35 treats
• Yoga space
• A pot with your treats in and your active and empty pot

1. Count out 20 treats and put them in the active pot with one in your hand ready.
2. Ask your dog to "sit".
3. Wait for any glance or side movement to the left (be patient).
4. Click even the slightest ear twitch or eye movement to the left.
5. Build this by clicking any repetitions and then begin to change your criteria so that

Jack is uneasy around Bubbles and uses a look away to communicate this.

only the most prominent looks to the left are clicked and treated. So the first thing you might click would be a flick of the left ear, but by the time you stop, an ear flick would be ignored and you should be only clicking a proper head turn.

6. Once you have got five consistent head turns left, take a break.

Follow the usual break protocol. This is intense learning; you want to keep it fun so don't be tempted to skip the break. Dog Yoga teaches dogs in a different way to conventional training. Even if your dog is still eager for the treats, he will learn better if you give him the opportunity to take in a little fresh air and have a drink. Remember it's the journey and not the destination that is important in learning. Don't focus too much on purist defined accomplishments; stay in the present and play at the training as if it's a game.

7. Count out ten more treats into the active pot to use, with one in your hand to get you started. We are going to start fine tuning.

8. Only click the longest head turns back. We are looking to increase this (over time and practice) to long glances. So every session where you practise this posture, aim for a long neck stretch. The head should be facing upwards not downwards so don't click downwards looks.

9. Now it is time to give the posture a name. So after three good repetitions start saying "stretch left". The action I usually use to accompany this is a slight head tilt (your head) to the right (the dog's left).

10. Now use the remaining five treats. The last five clicks will begin to build the duration. Hold off the click when your dog first glances back. Sometimes this will result in him doing the posture twice. If he does this then click the second one at its longest hold, and try to capture the longest duration you can without getting a repetition of the posture, where possible.

11. Each time you ask for the "stretch left" try to get your dog to hold the backwards neck stretch for longer until he is waiting for the click to release.

12. Only do this for five treats as it is a bit boring and requires hard concentration!

End of session – go play with your dog!

Neck stretch to the left.

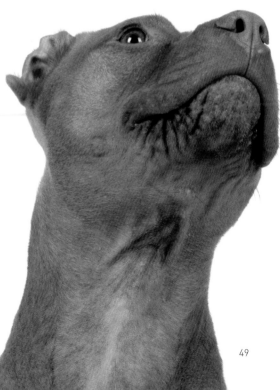

SESSION 1:4: SIT RIGHT NECK STRETCH ("STRETCH RIGHT")

What you will need:
- Clicker
- 70 treats
- Yoga space
- A pot with your treats in and an empty second pot

1. Count out 20 treats and put them in the active pot, with one in your hand to get you started.
2. Ask your dog to "sit".
3. Wait for any glance or side movement to the right – he will try the left first as he learnt this last time. Just hold out. You haven't given the command "stretch left" so you do

Neck stretch to the right.

not need to reward this previous behaviour. Don't be tempted – no matter how great the stretch – as this will only serve to confuse your dog!

4. Click even the slightest ear twitch to the right.
5. Build this by clicking any repetitions and then begin to change your criteria so that only the most prominent looks to the right are clicked and treated.
6. Once you have got five consistent head turns right, take a break.

Follow the usual break protocol and get a glass of water for yourself, too. This is intense learning and you want to keep it fun. The reason water and fresh air is important for you, and your dog, in training is that it rejuvenates your brain with oxygen. Oxygen to the brain is positive and gives the feeling of mental space, something which is vital for learning.

7. Count out ten more treats into the second pot with one in your hand to start.
8. Now only click the longest head turns right. We are looking to increase this (over time and practice) to long glances. So every session where you practise this posture, aim for a long neck stretch. The head should be facing upwards not downwards so don't click downwards looks.
9. Give the posture a name. So now after three good repetitions start saying "stretch right". The signal I use to accompany this is a slight head tilt to the left (the dog's right).
10. Count out five more treats into the second pot to use and put one in your hand to start.

11. The last five clicks will begin to build the duration, just as in the previous session, so hold off the click when your dog glances back right.
12. Each time try to get your dog to hold the backwards neck stretch for longer until he is waiting for the click to release.
13. Only do this for five treats.

Take a break, but as long as you are really enjoying the session and your dog is happy to continue then do some repeats!

1. Count out ten treats and put them in the second pot with one in your hand.
2. Ask your dog to "sit".
3. Ask your dog to "stretch left".
4. Click and build duration and posture strength of your stretch lefts.
5. Count out ten more treats.
6. Repeat the above steps but this time with your stretch rights.
7. Count out ten more treats.
8. Ask your dog to "sit".
9. Ask your dog clearly to "stretch left".
10. Click and treat.
11. Give him a second.
12. Now ask your dog to "stretch right".
13. Repeat, clicking and treating the postures and alternating them. Try putting in a few double stretch lefts or stretch rights to check that you have the same understanding.

This is a mammoth session – tons of praise and a big party for your dog is definitely needed after this one!

PAW RAISING

A natural paw raise is used differently by different dogs but, generally, whether it is to point at prey or at a potential predator, the paw raise marks that attention is being put upon something. A natural paw raise is done in a stand and can be subtle. Paw raises in Dog Yoga are not the same as this. They are stretches and should, eventually, aim to stretch the muscles in the upper as well as lower leg. While initially we will reward any paw raise delivered on cue, over time, as with all of the postures, we should aim for higher, longer and slower stretches which will increase body consciousness and control.

Ella raises her paw towards the new dog who interests her.

SESSION 1:5: SIT RIGHT PAW RAISE ("RIGHT FRONT")

What you will need:
• Clicker
• 30 treats
• Yoga space
• An active and a non-active pot

We can shape this behaviour or we can prompt it. Shaping is great with fidgety dogs and is my preferred way to teach it. However, it is harder and sometimes not so clear in terms of the dog's learning. If you have a dog who
is naturally a little slower or stationary, and who might just sit and not move his feet, then prompting the paw raise is far easier.

Try whichever way you feel will suit your dog best. If you are not getting paw action, you can try the other way. Prompting with a treat in the fist seems to be great for curious, confident, pushy dogs, whilst the shaping of the feet movement tends to work better with the more inhibited working or fearful and timid dogs.

SHAPING THE RAISE

1. Count ten treats into the active pot and put a treat in your hand to start.
2. Wait for a hint of movement on your dog's front right paw. This may be getting up or just adjusting his position.
3. Click and treat.
4. Repeat this ten times.
5. Count out another ten treats into your active pot and put a treat in your hand ready to start.
6. Click and treat when the paw rises from the ground and build up to as full an extension of the leg as possible.
7. Sometimes a dog will raise his other paw at the same time to increase the amount he can stretch and to help his balance; it's up to you whether you shape this out or not.
   If you want to shape it out, only click when one paw is fully extended and the other is on the ground. Don't click and reward if the left paw leaves the floor. Alternatively, just allow the dog to fully stretch and click so long as he is leading with the right paw. Both are fine versions of the posture for basic Dog Yoga.
8. Take a break with the usual break protocols.
9. Now use the remaining ten treats in your pot.
10. Build the extension of the leg and give the command a verbal cue.
11. Say "right front" as a verbal cue and then click and treat the best extensions.

THE OTHER WAY TO GET THE PAW...

1. Count ten treats into the pot to use and put a treat in both your hands to start.
2. Put one hand in a fist and present it to your dog, towards his paw.
3. Click each time he paws to get the treat. Then click and treat from the other hand.
4. Repeat.
5. Now count out ten more treats from the pot and present your fist, but much higher so that your dog can hardly reach it.

6. Click and treat each time your dog tries to pat your fist.
7. Raise your fist higher until he is pawing the air.
8. Take a break with the usual break protocols.
9. Now use the remaining ten treats in your second pot.
10. Build the extension of the leg and give the command a verbal cue.
11. Say "right front" as a verbal cue and then click and treat the best extensions.

Give your dog an enormous cuddle and a fun, runabout game to help him unwind after showing such awesome concentration!

SESSION 1:6. SIT LEFT PAW RAISE ("LEFT FRONT")

As above, but with the left paw instead.

If you and your dog are happy and are looking to carry on after a break (with the usual break protocol) then practise the following:

Prepare 30 treats and pop 10 in the active pot and 20 ready in the non active pot.

1. Place a treat in your hand ready with your clicker in the other.
2. Ask for "left front".
3. Hold off the click to see if you can get your dog to hold the paw up for longer and longer.

Left paw raise.

4. Click and treat.

5. Repeat ten times.

6. Now put ten more treats in the active pot and place one ready in your hand.

7. Ask for "right front". Hold off the click to see if you can get your dog to hold his paw up for longer and longer.

8. Click and treat.

9. Repeat ten times.

10. Now put the remaining treats in the active pot and place one ready in your hand.

11. Ask for "right front".

12. Click and treat.

13. Wait a few seconds.

14. Ask for "left front".

15. Click and treat.

16. Repeat steps 10-14 until you have no treats left.

Then give your dog a good old-fashioned wrestle-cuddle!

SESSION 1:7: SIT BOTH PAW RAISE ("BEG")

As is often the case, you will find plenty of different ways to teach a beg. When we are teaching a beg in this context, it is all about balance and duration. Using a stick or chair to begin with misses the point and doesn't emphasis body conscious movements or self-control, so bear with this technique and shape the behaviour instead. As the last sessions taught the front right and front left, your dog will probably paw strike initially anyway which will help. Give it a go!

What you will need:
• Clicker

• 40 treats
• Yoga space
• An active and a passive pot

1. Put ten treats into the active pot and one in your hand ready to train.

2. Wait and to begin with simply clicking and treating paw strikes.

3. Try to build towards only clicking when both paws are off the ground. You can do this by waiting and holding out when one comes up. Your dog will offer the other paw. If you only click after the left then right, or right then left paw is offered, he will begin to strike with both.

4. Count out a further ten treats into the active pot.

5. Now only click and treat both paws off the ground at the same time.

6. Count out ten treats into the active pot and pop one in your hand ready to add a verbal cue.

7. Say "beg".

8. Wait for both paws to lift off the ground.

9. Click and treat.

10. Repeat.

11. Take a break using the usual break protocol.

12. Use the remaining ten treats.

13. Ask for the "beg".

14. Begin to change your criteria so that you are emphasising the height of feet raising, then work on holding the click off for duration.

Hurray! You have completed your first set! Throw your dog a party of treats, praise and games and give him a day off tomorrow!

POSTURE RECAP SESSIONS

Now you have taught your first set, before teaching the second set you will want to practise. Practising behaviours should be done in two ways and recap sessions should take the following form:

• They should be done separately to teaching a new posture, expression or action but they can be done immediately before or after a training session (with a break in-between following break protocol).
• They should be done as per the outline below. No posture should be repeated more than ten times if you are not changing your criteria and not building on anything in a recap session. We don't want to ask for exactly the same thing ten times in a row as this is boring and demotivating.
• You can pick any posture taught to recap and, if you like, you can recap the same posture two or three days running. However, if your dog is struggling with a certain posture it may be beneficial to repeat the initial teaching process with that posture.

1. Pick one of the postures.
2. Get 15 treats and practise your chosen posture focusing on duration and pace. For example, with right front, left front and beg, we want the dog to raise his paws slowly. Get your dog to repeat the posture five times and watch his natural pace.
3. Now repeat this posture but only click and reward the ten slowest raises.
4. Now get 15 more treats and repeat the above, but this time focus on duration. Get your dog to practise the chosen posture five times clicking and rewarding each. Watch for how long he can stay in posture.
5. Now hold the click back and reward duration holds. The longer he can hold the posture, the better!

This can be done in exactly the same way with all the other sets, too.

Posture recap sessions give you the chance to fine tune.

CHAINING THE SET TOGETHER: CHAINING SESSIONS

Chaining is the process of linking different behaviours together in a sequence which is predictable for the dog. This makes them easier and even more relaxing to practise and so reinforces calmness and control. Think of links in a chain...

Eventually we want a sequence to be a fluid sequence of behaviours not dissimilar to dressage or even human tai-chi. It is possible to chain each of these behaviours together so that your dog will flow from one motion to the next, based upon your body cues. This is where the connection between dog and owner becomes a main feature in Real Dog Yoga.

What you will need:
• Clicker
• 20 treats
• Yoga space
• A pot with your treats in and an empty active pot

To begin you will just chain the sit and the stretch right together. So...
1. Ask your dog to "sit".
2. Wait five seconds.
3. Now ask him to "stretch right".
4. Click and throw a treat on the floor to release your dog from the posture.
5. Repeat ten times.
6. Now ask him to "sit" using only your hand signal. Use the slight head tilt and wait.

7. The moment he does a right stretch, click and throw the treat on to the floor
8. Repeat ten times.

So in your second chaining session you will repeat the above but adding in the third posture in the set.

For clarity, we will begin by using the words and the signals for all the postures. We do this as we want to make it easy and clear for your dog when we introduce new postures to a chained sequence.
1. Ask your dog to "sit".
2. Wait five seconds.
3. Now ask him to "stretch right".
4. Wait five seconds.
5. Now ask him to "stretch left".
6. Click and throw a treat on the floor to release your dog from the posture.
7. Repeat ten times.
8. Now ask him to "sit" using on your hand signal.
9. Use the slight left head tilt (the action we use to indicate right stretch) and wait.
10. Now use the slight right head tilt (the action we use to indicate left stretch) and wait.
11. The moment the dog does a left stretch, click and throw the treat on to the floor.
12. Repeat ten times but begin to wait so that after the sit, your dog offers the stretches on his own accord.
13. As soon as he is sitting then giving you a left and then right held neck stretch, give this sequence a name. Say "sequence sit" then wait for these three chained postures before you click and treat.

14. When you add the postures from this set, simply ask for them after asking for "sequence sit" and then repeat, fading the voice cue and then the hand cues until the posture becomes part of the sequence.

In each chaining session we add a new behaviour. Eventually we can practise the whole set with one voice cue. Remember, you might find the dog begins to rush specific postures. If your dog rushes then begin using a cue ("next") to indicate that it's time to change. This enhances a dog's focus and control and promotes exceptional connection training between trainer and dog. Again, practise this with the standing set and the down set once they are taught.

SESSION 2
THE STANDING SET

Teaching dogs different postures in stand is seldom done in any other form of training without motion. We teach motion actions in agility and motion postures in heelwork to music, but even in obedience we rarely see standing postures other than a straight stand. They are so important as actually, in real dog-dog interaction, they are what dogs use most. Compared to standing, we rarely ever see a dog sit in a natural environment to make poignant body language statements. With this in mind, teaching self and muscle control and relaxation in a stationary stand has obvious benefits.

In terms of training and practical use, practising the standing sequence helps with impulse control, recall, stop, slowing and leave-it type commands on a domestic level. For competitive sports, it promotes higher connection and body awareness and control.

The standing sequence – particularly the stretch left and stretch right, the front paw lifts, the tail motions and the sniff – can significantly help with reactive dogs. The gestures which, in natural circumstances are used to diffuse tension and promote passive negotiation seem to increase in natural behaviour when they are practised and reinforced in these sessions.

In addition, we can match and practice certain standing and down postures around potentially arousing things when completely under threshold. This must be practiced under the dog's emotional threshold and whilst slowly increasing the exposure of the frightening or frustrating stimuli.

This is explained in more detail in Section Three: Using Dog Yoga with dogs displaying challenging behaviour.

SESSION 2:1 STAND ("STAND")
What you will need:
• Clicker
• 25 treats
• Yoga space
• An active and a non-active pot

The majority of social interactions take place in a stand or while dogs are in motion.

1. Count out ten treats into the active pot and put one in your hand ready.
2. Click on your dog's approach as soon as he slows facing you.
3. Most dogs will immediately go into a sit, as the context now means that they will be worked in a sit (as per the last set).
4. Now, if you are patient and your dog has a good imagination, wait it out while he practises the sequences of behaviour that have in the past earned him treats. Wait for him to get up and quickly click and toss a treat for him to collect.
5. Alternatively.... I have found, particularly with obedience dogs, that some dogs find this impossible and will remain in the sit posture for hours. If this is the case, hold a treat in your hand and pop it under your dog's chest to lure him into a stand. Click and toss the treat on the floor.
6. Now repeat those steps, but if you chose to lure after a few repetitions, begin to move your hand out and just wait for the stand (this is called 'fading' the lure).

7. Take a break with the break protocols.

8. Count out a further ten treats.

9. Stand, hold your hand out in front of you, now hold it into a fist.

10. Your dog should sit.

11. Break the fist so that your hand moves from a fist to a horizontal line.

12. Wait for the stand.

13. Click and toss the treat away.

14. Repeat this ten times.

15. Have a break.

16. Now, with the remaining treats, repeat steps 8-13 but this time say "stand" just before you break your fist action into a horizontal line.

Good job! This is a new set so this is all a bit different and tricky. Give your dog a cuddle, play and scratch – that's enough work for today.

Stand.

SESSION 2:2

For the next session repeat your stand practice and build on duration.

1. Ask your dog to "stand".

2. Withhold the click when he stands and take a step away from him and then towards him.

3. Treat but do not click.

4. Repeat.

5. Repeat again but take two steps, then three then four.

Stand duration.

Build this up until you are walking around and around your dog, rewarding every now and then. Once your dog is capable of holding the stand while you move around the room, you can then move on to the standing stretch-left.

The release cue is the clicker and the word "ok". So say "ok", and click to release your dog out of the stand and then throw a treat on the floor to prompt the release.

Give your dog loads of fuss and let him out for a run!

SESSION 2:3: STAND RIGHT NECK STRETCH ("STRETCH RIGHT")

You will need:
• Clicker
• 30 treats
• Yoga space
• A non-active treat pot and an active one

Stand right neck stretches.

1. Count out ten treats.
2. Ask your dog to "stand".
3. Now again, you may find that some dogs find this exceedingly hard. This is often because we never ask dogs to do anything in a stationary, standing posture. We can help to cue the behaviour however, as the verbal and head cue may not yet be fully generalised – but we do need to be patient. That means that whilst the dog may understand "stretch right" in sit, he may not yet realise that it means the same thing when he is standing (or in a down). So we have to be patient and teach him this.
4. Ask for "stretch right", tilt your head as you do for the sitting stretch right and wait.
5. Click and treat even the flicker of movement in that right side of the head, and shape as per the sitting stretch right.
6. Repeat ten times.
7. Take a break with the usual break protocols (toilet and leg stretch for him, water, focus and stillness for you).
8. Now re-enter the Yoga space and count out ten more treats.
9. Repeat the above for ten clicks and shape for stretch (i.e. only click the best stretches). Alter your criteria in a way so that you are clicking and treating the best stretches of the neck, but don't expect more than your dog is capable of. You should still be clicking at least a quarter of the stretches being practised or your criteria is too high.
10. Take a break – this session is pretty gruelling!
11. Now count out your last ten treats.
12. Ask for the sitting "stretch right".
13. Hold, click and treat.

14. Now ask your dog to "stand".
15. Then ask for the standing "stretch right".
16. Hold, click and treat.

Phew! That was exhausting for you and your dog. Massive pats on backs all round. A good cuddle, plenty of water and a run is needed to shake that training off...

SESSION 2:4: STAND LEFT NECK STRETCH ("STRETCH LEFT")

You will need:
• Clicker
• 30 treats
• Yoga space
• A non-active treat pot and an active one

1. Count out ten treats and have one in your hand ready.
2. Ask your dog to "stand".
3. Usually – because you taught him the standing stretch left in your last session – your dog will try this posture to see if it still earns him a treat. Wait patiently and ask once for "stretch left"...wait...
4. Click and reward any hint of left side motion.
5. Repeat until you have used up your treats.
6. Take a break.
7. Re-enter your Yoga space and count out ten more treats with one in your hand ready.
8. Repeat the above for ten clicks and shape for the optimal stretch. Alter your criteria in a way that you are clicking and treating the best stretches of the neck. Remember not to expect too much too soon. and make sure you are doing lots of clicking!

9. Take another break as this session is hard.
10. Now count out the remaining treats.
11. Ask for a standing "stretch left".
12. Click and treat.
13. Ask for a sitting "stretch left".
14. Click and treat.
15. Ask for a sitting "stretch right".
16. Click and treat.
17. Ask for a standing "stretch right".
18. Click and treat.
19. Repeat, varying the order and repeating any that your dog seems to struggle with until there are no treats left.

You are nailing this! Good work by you and your dog so now both go and do something fun and easy together, ideally outside.

Stand left neck stretches.

SESSION 2:5: STAND HEAD LOOKING UP ("STRETCH UP")

You will need:

• Clicker
• 35 treats
• Yoga space
• A non-active treat pot and an active one

1. Count out ten treats and hold one ready in your hand.
2. While we could shape this, the neck arch that we want is slightly higher than is natural as we want the muscles to stretch. Therefore, luring is the best option to initiate the behaviour. Start by holding a treat above the dog's head.
3. Click the motion of him moving his head upwards.
4. Repeat for ten treats, slowly lifting your hand less and less and keeping it closer and close to your body.

Stand look up.

5. Count out ten more treats.
6. Now withdraw your hand and wait patiently.
7. Click and reward any move towards the upward stretch – and be patient!
8. Repeat for ten treats, beginning to click only the most obvious movement.
9. Take a break using the break protocol.
10. Count out 15 more treats.
11. Wait for the upward stretch, click and treat.
12. Repeat, clicking the best stretches.
13. Now point up and say "stretch up".
14. Wait.
15. Click and treat the stretches.
16. Repeat with the remainder of the treats.

Your done! This is a new form of concept learning so you should be delighted with progress. Make sure you give your dog a game in the garden or a cuddle as a relief from all that hard work...

SESSION 2:6: STAND HEAD TO FLOOR ("SNIFF")

What you will need:

• Clicker
• 55 treats
• Yoga space
• An active and non-active pot

1. Count out 20 treats into the active pot and put one in your hand ready.
2. Put a treat on the floor and click as soon as your dog's nose hits it.
3. Reward him out of your hand as well
4. Repeat this five times.
5. Count out ten more treats.
6. Now point to the floor.
7. Click as soon as your dog puts his nose to the ground (some dogs get this straight

THE REAL DOG YOGA

away and others take much longer. Be patient, there is no rush!).

8. Repeat this ten times.

9. Count out ten more treats.

10. Now begin asking "sniff" and just point at the floor.

11. Wait.

12. Click and treat every time your dog chooses to touch the floor following your verbal cue.

13. Take a break.

14. Now with the remaining 15 treats you are going to begin clicking for duration.

15. Ask for the "sniff" and point to the floor.

16. Hold the click off just a fraction of a second. If your dog comes up and looks for the treat, wait and click the second time. Next time you will have to be quicker and increase duration by smaller increments.

17. Keep going until you have used up all your treats.

That's enough of the head action – now for the feet! Make sure you give your dog a little jackpot. Try throwing a handful of treats across the lawn and letting him sniff them out as a relaxing treat game after such hard work.

PAW RAISING

Remember with the paw raises that a little paw raise is fine when the dog is standing. Without momentum of movement and without the balance of sitting, the paw lifts are bound to be less extended than in the sitting set – that is why we call them paw raises rather than paw stretches. The muscles in the leg are worked via slow and careful movement, and balance and body awareness in increased.

SESSION 2:7: STAND RIGHT PAW RAISE ("RIGHT FRONT")

You will need:
• Clicker
• 40 treats
• Yoga space
• A non-active treat pot and an active one

1. Count 20 treats into the active pot and hold one in your hand ready.

2. Ask your dog to "sit".

3. As you have been working on head postures the last few sessions, your dog will find it hard to move his consciousness towards another part of his body so you need to set him up for success. I would suggest going through the paw raises in the sitting set first.

4. Practise five left and five right sitting paw stretches.

5. Ask your dog to "stand".

6. Ask for "right front". If he sits to give you the right front, don't click. Simply ask him to stand, treat (but don't click) the stand, and repeat.

Stand head to floor.

7. Click and treat any right paw movement until you finish the treats up.
8. Now take a break and have a lovely, cool glass of water, etc.
9. Count out a further ten treats.
10. Ask your dog to "stand".
11. Click and treat right paw movements.
12. As the paw motions start, begin to shape and only click the best right paw lifts.
13. Repeat until you have used up the treats in the active pot.
14. Count out the last ten treats.
15. Ask for "sit right front" and click and treat.
16. Now ask for "stand right front" and click and treat.
17. Repeat until you have used all ten treats.

Wow! Awesome session... So much concentration needed on both
your parts so you should feel super proud.

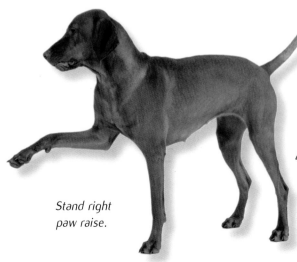

*Stand right
paw raise.*

SESSION 2:8: STAND LEFT PAW RAISE ("LEFT FRONT")

Remember that dogs are left or right pawed. Females are more likely to be right pawed and males are more likely to be left pawed! This is worth bearing in mind as asking for the non-dominant paw to be raised is a little like asking a right-handed person to write a letter with their left hand. One paw will be much harder for your dog to use than the other. That said, it means that learning to control and use the non-dominant paw more effectively, has real value. It can be really useful in improving balance and level movement in both agility and obedience.

What you will need:
• Clicker
• 40 treats
• Yoga space
• A non-active pot (with your treats in) and an active pot

1. Count out 20 treats and put them ready in your active pot. Get one in your hand ready.
2. Ask your dog to "stand".
3. Now ask for "left front". He may just give you his other paw as this was the last thing you practised. Remember: no matter how brilliant those right fronts are, don't reinforce them as this is not what you have asked for.
4. Click and treat any motion with the other paw. Some dogs get this really quickly. If your dog is struggling, ask for a sitting "right front" and a sitting "left front", then ask him to stand and try again.

5. Repeat, clicking the best, most confident left fronts.
6. Take a break. If it's winter then give your dog a cuddle outside of the Yoga space. If it is the summer then why not join him outside with your drink.
7. Now count out ten more treats.
8. Ask for the "left front".
9. Click and treat the posture.
10. Repeat ten times.
11. Count out the remaining ten treats.
12. Now ask for "left front" and "right front", alternately clicking and treating the paw lifts.

All finished – hurray! Throw your puppy a party. You are about half way through the standing set now but, be warned, the next few postures are taxing...

Stand left paw raise.

SESSION 2:9: STAND BACK RIGHT PAW RAISE ("RIGHT BACK")

As with the front paw raises, we have to be super quick with the clicker. This is really tough shaping so to get these postures you will have to be confident about using that clicker properly. If in doubt, get a tennis ball and practise clicking some bounces before your start!

Take a long deep breath. Be clear about what you are training and take it one step at a time. If you are not ready to move on, think of ways to break the exercise down further – and never be afraid of adding treats to the pot. Remember that it is a process to enjoy so work through the steps, but do break off if you or your dog are getting frustrated.

What you will need:
• Clicker
• 45 treats
• Yoga space
• A non-active pot and an active pot. Remember that the active one is only for treats we are currently using and saves you getting your hands all treaty!

1. Count out 15 treats and get one in your hand ready to use.
2. Ask for a "stand".
3. Now hold a treat slightly in front of your dog, close by his chest, as though asking him to move backwards.
4. Click when the back right paw steps back.
5. Treat in front of your dog. So just as he moves his back leg click then treat just in front. This makes it clearer that you don't want him to move back.

6. Repeat five times.
7. Now, wait and see if your dog will offer a step back, or a movement with his right back paw.
8. Click and treat any back right motions until you have used up the remaining ten treats.
9. Take a break.
10. Now count out another 15 treats.
11. Wait for the right back leg motions and click and treat the first five.
12. Now only click the good ones with the remaining ten treats.
13. Count out a further ten treats.
14. Now say "right back" and point behind to the back right of your dog.
15. Wait...
16. Click and treat those movements, shaping to get the very best right raises.
17. Shape out any movement back or forward by only clicking the most stationary back paw lifts.

Back left paw raise.

Whoop whoop! That was really tricky so give yourself a pat on the back and your dog a massive cuddle.

SESSION 2:10: STAND BACK LEFT PAW RAISE ("LEFT BACK")

What you will need:
• Clicker
• 50 treats
• Yoga space
• Two pots as usual (non-active and active)

1. Count out ten treats and hold one in your hand ready.
2. Ask for a "stand".
3. Now lure your dog back a step again, like last time, but this time you are clicking and treating the left back leg moving.
4. Repeat this ten times.
5. Count out 15 treats.
6. Now remove the lure and wait for the left paw to move.
7. Click and treat any left paw motion.
8. Repeat this for five treats.
9. Now begin only clicking and treating the best paw raises. Remember to be realistic with your criteria – don't try to fully extend if your dog is only just getting the idea of left back paw movements.
10. Take a break.
11. Now count out ten more treats.
12. Ask "left back" and point to the back left of your dog.
13. Click and treat back left paw raises.
14. Now use the remaining treats to practise front right, front left, back left and back right standing paw raises.

Bet you didn't think you would be able to teach your dog such control! Lots of praise for both you and him! The next four are slightly easier to teach...

TAIL CONTROL

Like cats, dogs have lots of different uses for their tails. First off, they need them for balance. A dog is capable of incredible leaps and jumps and he rarely slips or falls. The tail lifts and lowers to keep him balanced. Additionally, dogs use their tails to communicate – and it is so much more complicated than wagging when happy, and between the legs when sad.

The height of the tail's position can read a little bit like a meter for arousal. Mid-tail postures usually signal a relaxed, happy dog. A high tail signals an alert and aroused dog, and a low tail signals a distressed and frightened dog.

The speed of the wag also denotes excitement levels. Giorgio Vallortigora,

a neuroscientist in Italy, led a team that studied the significance of directional bias in dog tail wags. Their research suggested that dogs wag their tail more to the left when they are under threat, and more to the right when they are relaxed.

Dogs have entire conversations with their tails, so teaching them muscle control here is really great. However, these cues are hard to teach. You have to be very patient; watch for signs of frustration and change your pace and reward frequency if you see it.

SESSION 2:11: STAND TAIL LIFT ("TAIL LIFT")

What you will need:
• Clicker
• 65 treats
• Yoga space (still clean and tidy remember!)
• Two pots, one active and one non-active

1. Count 20 treats and put them in the active

Ella has her tail tense and low as she is a little worried about Marley. In contrast, Marley's tail is wagging and high showing he is excited and wants to play.

pot.

2. Now, you are not going to ask your dog to do anything here. You are going to capture the tail lift. To begin with if your dog lifts his tail while he is moving, click and treat.

3. Be still and wait for your dog. If he keeps sitting, ask for a "stand".

4. Click any suggestion of a tail move. At this stage, you can click left, right, up or down tail movements.

5. Click 20 tail movements. Keep the reinforcement really quick. That means your criteria for movement should be low. Tiny tail movements should be reinforced for a while. Don't start asking for more – or for specific tail movements – until you are

certain your dog understands that you are clicking his tail moving. This could take some time so be patient, cool, calm and forgiving (of yourself and of your dog).

6. Now count out 20 more treats.

7. You are going to do pretty much the same again, but now you need to begin to really focus on upward tail movement. If it's up to the left or to the right, that's fine – but don't click the tail moving downwards.

8. Begin to shape the tail up, so only click bigger movements and movements where the tail is moving upwards – lifting.

9. Take a break – a very, very well-earned break. If you are feeling frustrated or your dog is finding this super hard then, when you return, practise some of the other postures and leave moving on until tomorrow.

10. Count out 15 more treats.

11. Start increasing your shaping criteria as you begin to give the command "tail lift", and then wait.

12. Click and treat the tail going up.

13. Now start asking for the tail lift. Only click when the dog is stationary and lifts his tail.

14. Repeat until your active pot is empty.

15. Take a short break; you don't need to follow precise break protocol here. Just give yourself and your dog a moment to shake all this off and have a drink.

16. With the remainder of the treats, practise asking for the "tail lift".

17. Click and treat.

18. If your dog has really 'got it', intersperse different standing postures.

Phew! That was a mega sesh! Cool down and make sure you and your dog get a really good night's sleep!

Stand tail lift.

SESSION 2:12 STAND TAIL DROP ("TAIL DROP")

What you will need
- Clicker
- Yoga space
- 60 treats
- Two pots as usual

1. Do not fear, this one is easier now you have the tail lift.
2. Count out 20 treats.
3. Ask for a "stand", then for a "tail lift".
4. Reward both, but click neither. Wait until the tail begins to drop.
5. Click the tail dropping, treat and praise your dog.
6. Repeat this ten times.
7. Now stop treating or asking for the tail lift. Only click and treat the tail going down.
8. Repeat ten times. In between each, once you have clicked, toss the treat to reward your dog. In this way he will have to reposition each time (otherwise you will end up with a dog just standing in front of you all confused!).
9. Count out ten more treats.
10. This time, so long as your dog is ready (if he isn't, continue the above for ten more treats until he is), click and treat the tail drop – but give the treat directly to his mouth.
11. Repeat ten times.
12. Break time! Take the usual break, and clear the space and your head. Hopefully, your dog will clear his head, too. Enjoy the stillness, clarity and water.
13. Ready? Count out 20 more treats.
14. Ask your dog to stand (treat but don't click).
15. Now say "tail drop".
16. Click and treat the tail dropping.

Stand tail drop.

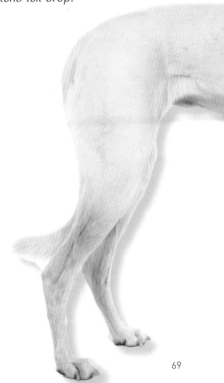

17. Start to click and treat proper tail drops only, so you can move your criteria as to where on the back legs the dog is dropping his tail. If it is a half-drop, just wait and see if he will offer something a little more. But remember, if your dog begins to get frustrated reduce your criteria and increase the frequency of treat-giving.
18. Repeat until you have run out of treats.
19. Count out the remaining ten treats and have one ready.
20. Now ask for a "tail lift".
21. Click and treat.
22. Ask for a "tail drop".
23. Click and treat.

Brilliant! Another marathon session out the way! Lots of games and cuddles for your dog. You are doing so well. Tail postures are really hard...

Stand tail wag

SESSION 2:13 STAND TAIL WAG ("WAG IT")

What you will need:
• Clicker
• Yoga space
• 45 treats
• Two pots (active and non active). Put all the treats in one pot then count out the treats you are using into the active pot so that you don't have to think about numbers while you train.

1. This is super easy for most dogs. To begin, count out ten treats.
2. Now, clap your hands and say "wag it!" in an excitable voice.
3. A little excitement is okay here, but not too much, so tailor your excitement level to your dog.
4. Click tail wags very early on.
5. Slowly reduce your excitement over the course of ten treats.
6. Count out ten more treats.
7. Stop any form of clap or action and just say "wag it!" in a moderately excited voice.
8. Click and treat wags. Remember, during this set we don't want too much excitement or the dog will find it hard to concentrate, control and learn. That said, we do want a little bit as it is great for your dog to learn to get a little bit excited and then come back down.
9. No need for a break really as this should be quite fun and easy, so keep asking, clicking and treating until there are no treats left in your active pot.
10. Now count out ten more treats and go low key. Say "wag it!" Be patient and click and treat left-right movements.

11. Shape it up: click the most dramatic movements and don't be afraid to hold back your click until you get a better wag, so long as you are sure your dog knows what you are asking.
12. Keep going until there are no treats left in your active pot.
13. Count out the remainder of the treats. This next step is harder for your dog so be patient, calm, super clear and forgiving.
14. Ask for "tail lift".
15. Click and treat.
16. Ask for "tail drop".
17. Click and treat.
18. Ask for "wag it".
19. Click and treat.
20. Repeat until there are no treats.

Guess what? You have sorted out another whole set! So now you have the whole first and second sets. Well done! Now take a week off training new behaviours and work on chaining and repetitions. Spend the time playing and perhaps doing a little practice of the postures you have already trained. But give yourself and your dog a week off new information.

SESSION 3
THE DOWN SET

When your dog is chilled and relaxed he lies down. We all like dogs that are chilled and relaxed so the more reinforcement we can give for the down postures, the better!

In terms of social learning it is also really great to help our dogs to control varying down postures. When dogs are uncomfortable they negotiate distance from things using their head and paws. This is even true when they are in the down position, particularly when they are guarding a resource, a valuable space or themselves (especially if they are in physical discomfort).

When two dogs lie together, you often see them appropriately adjust their proximity so that they are facing away from one another or looking away. This can be interpreted as a reasonable posturing that just says: "Nah - I don't want a cuddle mate", and can be seen to prevent aggressive displays. Dogs also use the

When dogs are relaxed they often lie down to rest.

down (rolling) actions and movements to show sheer abandonment (pleasure) or sometimes to self-calm and de-escalate.

The down set is hugely important and particularly promotes relaxation. It is important if we are practising these postures around things that have caused anxiety in the past to be very, very aware of proximity. If you are doing this sort of work ensure you have the advice of a professional so that you are entirely aware of where your dog's emotional thresholds are (see Section Three for further information).

SESSION 3:1: DOWN ("DOWN")

After your week-long holiday, let's begin with something easy!

What you will need:
• Clicker
• Yoga space (with mat)
• Treats
• Two pots (active and non-active)

1. Count out ten treats (have two in your hand ready to start).
2. Ask your dog to "sit" (treat but do not click).
3. Slowly take the other treat in front of your dog's nose and pull it slowly, slowly down.
4. Click as your dog lowers, and feed the treat from your hand on to the floor.
5. Repeat this, lowering your dog further and further (if you are struggling try moving the treat further away in front of your dog).
6. Count out ten more treats.
7. Once your dog is actively following the treat into the down position, start fading your treat lure.
8. Remove the treat from your lure hand and just lower your hand to the floor (keeping the treat in your other hand and away).
9. Then give the treat to your dog in between his paws, in the down, after a click.
10. Repeat five times.
11. Now begin to reduce the amount your hand has to go down. For the next five times, decrease the action until you are just pointing down.
12. Take a break with all the usual break protocols. It might be worth rereading the section on break protocols again just to refresh.
13. Count out ten more treats.
14. Point down and say "down".
15. Click and treat when your dog goes down.

Down.

SETTLE

The settle is a fantastic command to use in place of a down when we are wanting a dog to relax. We can set up a context but also use commanding postures to help him understand what is desirable to us. For example, if I go to the cafe with my dogs and I get a coffee, I'll throw something comfortable for them to sleep on (set up the context), and ask for a settle (a posture complicit with what I want them to do). This makes it very clear that I want them to relax, and not go into a down, which is the posture dogs can take to pounce in their predatory-prey sequence.

Remember to use the 'it pays to stay' method with your down postures in order to teach duration.

SESSION 3:2: SETTLE RIGHT ("SETTLE RIGHT")

What you will need:

- Clicker
- Treats
- Two pots
- Yoga space with a mat

1. Count out ten treats.
2. Ask for a "down" (treat but do not click).
3. With a treat in your hand, lure your dog's head slightly to turn to the left. Hold it until the hip moves just slightly and the dog is propped on his right side.
4. Click and treat.
5. Repeat until you have no treats left in your active pot.
6. Count out ten more treats.
7. Ask for the "down" and then wait...
8. Click, treat and praise up your dog when he moves on to his right hip.
9. Repeat until you have used up ten treats.
10. Take a break!
11. Count out a further ten treats.
12. Now this time ask for "settle right".
13. Wait and click and treat when your dog moves into the right settle position.
14. Repeat until you have no treats left in you active pot.
15. Count out the remaining treats (there should be ten left but if there's 11 or nine don't worry!).
16. Ask for a "down".
17. Click and treat.
18. Ask for a "settle right". It might take a little longer for your dog to work back into the down from the settle right so be patient and wait it out.

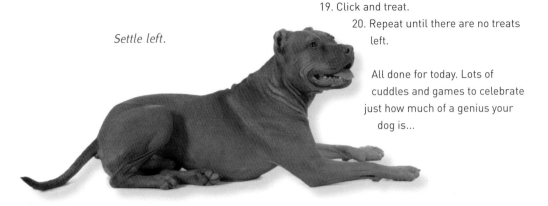

Settle left.

19. Click and treat.
20. Repeat until there are no treats left.

All done for today. Lots of cuddles and games to celebrate just how much of a genius your dog is...

3:3: SETTLE LEFT ("SETTLE LEFT")

Remember the left/right bias we talked about earlier? Dogs prefer their left or right just as we are left and right-handed. This holds true for right and left settles, so be aware that your dog will find settling on one side easier than the other. Just be patient. Ensure you offer your dog breaks if he is getting frustrated, and remember to break things down into easier chunks if he is struggling.

What you will need:
• Clicker
• 40 treats
• Two pots (one with treats in and one to count treats you're going to use directly into)
• Yoga space with a mat

1. Count out ten treats.
2. Ask your dog to go into a "down" on the mat.
3. Now hold a treat in your hand and lure your dog to look round and down to the right.
4. Hold the treat there and click and reward

Settle right.

from the non-lure hand) when your dog settles on to his left side.

5. Repeat until you have used all your active treats.
6. Now count out ten more treats.
7. Ask for "settle left".
8. Be patient and wait for your dog to settle left. If he finds it hard you can ask for the down to help him the first few times.
9. Repeat for ten treats.
10. Take a break...then...
11. Count out the remaining 20 treats.
12. Ask for "settle left".
12. Click and treat.
13. Ask for down...be patient. If it's too hard take a treat in your hand, find your dog's nose and move the treat forward, luring him to alter his posture.
14. Click and treat the down.
15. Now ask for "settle right".
16. Again, this might be hard and you should use clear hand signals to help your dog. Be patient and click and treat the settle right.
15. Repeat the whole thing until there are no treats left.

With both settles sorted, it is time for a good old ear scratch and cuddle...

SESSION 3:4: DOWN WITH HEAD ON PAWS ("SAD")

What you will need:
• Clicker
• 45 treats
• Yoga space
• Two pots; one with all the treats in (non-active) and an active one to use.

1. Count out ten treats.
2. Ask for the "down".
3. Put a treat in your closed hand and hold the treat to the floor between your dog's front paws.
4. Click and reward with the other hand every time your dog's nose touches between his paws until you have used up all ten treats.
5. Count out 15 treats.
6. Ask for a "down".
7. This time, don't have a treat in your hand but put your hand level with your dog's head, point to the floor and say "sad".
8. Wait.
9. Click and treat any time your dog moves his head down.
10. Shape this until you are only clicking when your dog has his head touching the floor between his paws.

Down with head on paws (centre).

11. Take a break here if you feel your dog would benefit from one – but it's not too intense...
12. Count out ten treats.
13. Ask for "sad" and just point (from where you are stationed) at the floor.
14. Click and treat your dog for putting his head down.
15. Count out ten more treats.
16. Ask for "sad".
17. This time, hold off the click to try to build up the time your dog keeps his head on the floor.
18. If he breaks the "sad", don't reward. Ask for it again and lower your duration criteria a little bit next time.
19. Repeat until you are out of treats.

Now that wasn't too taxing, but it still deserves a fun game outside and lots of cuddles for your dog.

SESSION 3:5: DOWN WITH HEAD DROPPED TO THE LEFT ("SAD LEFT")

Whilst option shaping is preferable in most of the Real Dog Yoga training, this posture is much easier to lure.

That said, feel free to shape the sad left instead, if you want to. To do this you can ask for the standard sad, and then shape it to the left by only clicking and treating when the head goes further and further to the left. When the left head slant is significant, give it a new name. Alternatively, you can do this with a lure which is, I think, easier for most dogs.

What you need:
• Clicker
• Two pots
• Yoga space
• 40 treats

1. Count ten treats out and get one in your hand.
2. Ask for the "sad", but this time point to the left hand side of the dog with your treat hand.
3. Wait patiently for your dog's head to touch the floor.
4. When it does, click and treat with your other hand.
5. Repeat five times.
6. Take the treat from your hand and repeat a further five times.
7. Count out ten more treats.
8. Now begin to move your hand up further when you ask, and point down and to the left.
9. Click and treat when your dog's head touches the left of his paw.
10. Keep this up until you have used up all your treats, clicking and rewarding the best sad left postures.
11. Take a break.

Down with head on paws left.

12. When you return, count out ten more treats.
13. Say "sad left", wait...
14. Click and treat the sad left posture.
15. Now repeat, but begin to hold off the clicks and work on duration.
16. Count out ten more treats.
17. Ask for the "sad"...wait...click and treat.
18. Now ask for the "sad left"...wait...if your dog gives you a standard sad, just hold off and wait until he appropriates his head posture.
19. Click and treat.
20. Repeat until there are no treats left.

All done! Pat on the back for you – and a cuddle and a fuss for your super smart pooch.

SESSION 3:6: DOWN WITH HEAD DROPPED TO THE RIGHT ("SAD RIGHT")

As I have already intimated, it is useful to keep in mind the fact that your dog will have a left or a right hand bias. Remember this because it will make it harder to teach certain commands.

For those commands it is best to increase the frequency with which you reinforce, and do not be frightened or concerned that it may take slightly longer. I would usually recommend that when you are aware of your dog's bias (e.g. if you find that he or she prefers the left hand side), that you always teach postures on his 'best' side first.

What you will need:
• Clicker
• Two pots (active and non-active)
• Yoga space
• 30 treats

1. Count out ten treats into your active pot and hold one in your hand.
2. Ask your dog into the "sad" posture (reward with a treat but not a click).
3. Ask for the "sad left" and reward (but no clicks).
4. Now point to the right of your dog and ask for "sad right"...wait...
5. Many dogs will be able to get this now so make sure you give them time and space to work it out.
6. If your dog struggles then point lower to the ground.

Using targets improves clarity for your dog.

7. Click and treat when then nose touches the ground and repeat.
8. Count out ten more treats.
9. Ask for "sad right".
10. Click and treat the posture, fading your pointing hand until it is in the usual position and your dog is listening to the "sad right" suggestion.
11. Count out ten more treats.
12. Click and treat for duration so work hard to try to get your dog to keep his head down there, holding on for the click!
13. Repeat until there are no treats left.

Yey! Head postures are nailed! Remember,- you can always go back and practise postures whenever you like. Every session should be progressive with tangible criteria – but that doesn't mean new postures have to be part of every session.

SESSION 3:7: DOWN WITH RIGHT PAW FORWARD ("RIGHT FRONT")

What you will need:
- Clicker
- Treats
- Two pots (active and passive)
- Yoga space

- A target (A target can be anything really but I would suggest that you cut out a square of coloured paper and put some Bluetac on the back. If you have a destructive or easily frustrated dog you may want to stick it down with clear tape instead of Bluetac).

1. Take a nice deep breath and ensure that you are in the right place mentally, to train.
2. Count out ten treats.
3. Put your target in your hand.
4. Hold it out towards your dog (but not in his face) and click and treat every time his right paw touches it. You can ask for "right front" as this will help.
5. Ask him to "sit" and then go again.
6. Ask him to "stand" and repeat.
7. Count out five more treats.
8. Ask your dog to "down" (you can treat but do not click).
9. Put your target in front of your dog's right paw and ask for "right front". Click and treat every time he paws the target.
10. Count out five more treats.

Down right paw forward.

11. Put the target on the floor in front of your dog's right paw. Wait until your dog offers a right front then click and treat.

12. Repeat this until there are no treats in the active pot.

13. Take a break with all the usual protocols.

14. Count out ten treats.

15. Cut or rip the target in half.

16. Ask for "down" then "front right".

17. Click and treat.

18. Repeat this, each time cutting the target in half until it is barely there.

19. Count out ten treats.

20. Remove the target.

21. Ask for "front right".

22. Click and treat that paw moving forward in front.

23. Repeat until you have no treats left - shaping the most prominent paw motions.

Great concept learning. This is the first posture taught with a target and you and your dog mastered it!

SESSION 3:8 DOWN WITH LEFT PAW FORWARD ("LEFT FRONT")

What you will need:
- Clicker
- 35 treats
- Two pots (active and passive)
- Yoga space
- A target

1. Count out ten treats.

2. Ask your dog to "down" (you can treat but do not click.)

3. Put your target in front of your dog's left paw and ask for "left front".

4. Repeat and only click when your dog hits the target with his left paw. This should be easy considering yesterday you taught exactly the same command with the right paw.

5. Count out five more treats.

6. Wait until your dog offers a left front target and click and treat.

Down left paw forward.

7. Repeat this until there are no treats in the pot.
8. Take a break with all the usual protocols.
9. Count out ten treats.
10. Cut or rip the target in half.
11. Ask for "left front".
12. Click and treat
13. Repeat this, each time cutting the target in half until it is barely there.
14. Count out ten treats.
15. Remove the target.
16. Ask for "left front".
17. Repeat until you have no treats left.

All done! Getting that paw awareness in the down set is quite tricky and in the next session it gets even harder so make sure you have a good mental warm down today. Perhaps a relaxing stroll and sniff, or a fun game.

SESSION 3:9: DOWN WITH PAWS CROSSED ("CROSS THEM")

Down with paws crossed.

This is a cool little dance move for your dog, but it is also a good Dog Yoga posture. Initially the postures started with a left over right cross and a right over left cross. However, when practising this, it became very apparent that the left/right paw bias made it uncomfortable and quite frustrating for a dog. When looking at the postures, it is so important that your dog is comfortable and relaxed. While a left front or right front (depending on the dog's bias), is initially hard to get, it seems that afterwards a dog finds it easy and comfortable to deliver. The same cannot be said of the crossing-paws so, for this posture, allow your dog to show you which paw cross is the most comfortable for him, and use that one.

What you will need:
• A clicker
• A target
• Yoga space
• Two pots
• 40 treats

1. Count out ten treats.
2. Ask for a "down".
3. Place the target at the top of one of the paws.
4. Allow the dog to choose which paw he paws the target with and click and treat.
5. Repeat this, gently moving the target further and further towards the other paw until the paw has to touch the other paw in order to touch the target.
6. Count out ten treats.
7. Now hold the target in your hand by, or over, the opposite paw and ask for "cross them".
8. We are cueing the dog to lift his paw up, and to the other side, to get the target.

9. Repeat this until the paw is crossing the other paw – as soon as the cross happens click, treat and really praise your dog.

10. Now count out ten more treats.

11. Place the target on the opposite side of the dog's paw so that the dominant paw will have to cross the other one to get it... wait....

12. Click, treat and throw a party when your dog crosses his paws.

13. This is a tricky one so use the target carefully and make sure you are changing your criteria in realistic, incremental changes. Remember that fools rush in, and that this should be an enjoyable if tricky process of non-pressured learning.

14. Take a break.

15. Once you have got this far, you can count ten treats and carefully begin cutting the target in half.

16. Ask for "cross them".

17. Click and treat the crossed paw.

18. Now repeat, each time cutting the target in half until you can remove it.

19. Last little bit is the duration, so count out your last batch of ten treats.

20. Now ask for "cross them" and hold off the click.

21. Each time hold it off for a teeny bit longer, but not so as to frustrate the dog or break the posture.

That was a real toughie. Good job on your part as both learning facilitator and student. I'm sure you will agree that your dog did a great job learning as well as teaching you, too. Appreciate each other and praise all round.

SESSION 3: 10 DOWN LYING FLAT (RIGHT) ("FLAT RIGHT")

We always use option shaping for postures like the last three of the down set. These last three involve the dog choosing to position himself in a way which is fundamentally vulnerable. It is so important when teaching these positions to respect your dog's feelings. We don't want to ask him to do something which doesn't make him feel good, so be very aware of body language with these ones. We also try not to ask for much in the way of duration with these for the same reason – so don't ask your dog to lie flat for hours!

Flat right.

What you will need:
- A clicker
- A mat (laid out at the beginning of the session for dogs tht find laying on hard surfaces unpleasant)
- 30 treats
- Yoga space
- Two pots (active and non-active)

1. Take ten treats from the non-active pot and put nine of them in the active pot ready to use. Put one in your hand.
2. Ask your dog to "right settle" (treat but do not click).
3. Ask your dog to "left front" (treat but do not click).
4. Use a treat as a lure in your hand to lure the dog's head down gently and back to the right until he is lying nearly on his side.
5. Click and treat when a significant part of him alters to move his body on to his side.
6. Repeat this, each time raising your criteria in small increments until your dog is moving predominantly on to his side.
7. Count out ten more treats.
8. Repeat the above ten times, but begin presenting a flat hand tilted to the right as opposed to luring the dog's head down and back.
9. At the same time start introducing the verbal cue: "flat right". Remember that the verbal cue should come just before the action is clickable.
10. Fade the hand signal until you can do it from your usual training situ.
11. Take a break.
12. Count out ten more treats.
13. Ask your dog to "down".
14. Click and treat.
15. Ask your dog to "settle right".

16. Click and treat.
17. Ask him to "settle left".
18. Click and treat.
19. Ask him to "flat right"...wait...
20. Click and treat.
21. Repeat in various orders until there are no treats left.

This is a tough one. Getting the initial posture can be hard for the dog to understand. It needs trust and patience on both sides, so well done.

SESSION 3:11 DOWN LYING FLAT (LEFT) ("FLAT LEFT")

What you will need:
- A clicker
- A mat
- Yoga space
- Two pots
- 40 treats

1. Take ten treats and get one in your hand.
2. Ask your dog to "left settle" (treat but do not click).
3. Ask your dog to "right front" (treat but do not click).
4. Use a treat in your hand to lure the dog's head down gently and back to the left until he is lying nearly on his side. Don't force it, just offer the treat and do it more and more in small incremental changes.

Flat left.

5. Click and treat when a significant part of him alters to move his body on to his side.
6. Repeat this, each time raising your criteria until your dog is moving predominantly on to his left side.
7. Count out ten more treats.
8. Repeat this process ten times, but begin using a hand gesture as opposed to luring the dog's head.
9. At the same time start introducing the verbal cue: "flat left".
10. Fade the hand signal until you can do it from your usual training position.
11. Take a break.
12. Count out 20 more treats.
13. Ask your dog to "down".
14. Click and treat.
15. Ask your dog to "settle right'.
16. Click and treat.
17. Ask him to "settle left".
18. Click and treat.
19. Ask him to "flat right".
20. Click and treat.
21. Ask him to "down".
22. Click and treat.
23. Ask him to "flat left".
24. Click and treat.
25. Repeat in various orders until there are no treats left.

Well done! Make sure that the warm down is something fun that you both enjoy – a scatter feed, or perhaps a snuggle on the sofa.

SESSION 3:12 DOWN ON THE BACK ("OVER")

This is the third and most vulnerable flat-out posture. Be highly vigilant for signs of stress and if you feel that your dog is not feeling at ease and comfortable (i.e. that his body is stressed, muscles are rigid or that he feels unhappy in the position) then stop and come back to it another time after your dog has been practising the other lie flat postures for a longer period of time.

What you will need
• Clicker
• Mat
• A Yoga space
• Two pots
• 40 treats

1. Count out ten treats
2. Ask your dog into the "flat left" or "flat right" (whichever he finds easier).
3. Using a food lure in your hand allow your dog to nibble at the treat as you move it up, so that he begins to appropriate his body and turn his belly upwards.
4. Repeat this clicking and rewarding by tossing the treat on the floor so that your dog has to get to his feet to reach the treat and then get back into posture again for the next treat.

Over.

5. Count out ten more treats.

6. Repeat the above but start asking for "over" as you lure your nibbling dog to turn from flat left to flat right or visa-versa

8. Right, now take the treat out of the hand and start fading the luring hand. To do this first use the empty hand exactly as you did before but without a treat in it.

9. Now hold the empty hand higher each time you ask for "over" until you can ask for the "over" from your normal training situ without a lure hand.

10. Take a break.

11. Count out ten treats and take a deep breath.

12. Ask for "over" and signal to your dog

13. Wait patiently and if you have to, shape the posture. To do this, click and treat anything remotely like the over posture and increase your criteria until you have a full over posture, clicking when the dog is belly-up and on his back.

15. Repeat this until your dog is happily moving into the over posture on cue.

And you are done! All the postures – all of them – all three sets! Gosh! A few days off is what is needed. Play, do scent games and have loads of brilliant cuddles with your dog. You can practise the various postures in the garden or the park, but you should take it slow and easy and make sure you are both enjoying it!

Teaching dogs to move carefully and with control is tricky but extremely useful. It requires impulse control and focus. It brings up arousal slightly in a controlled manner while maintaining a steady focus of the mind. Teaching spins and circles can be great in terms of warming up working dogs, too, increasing body awareness, including backend awareness. All this, of course, underpins a steady control of the senses. These are particularly useful when practised around distractions, out and about, as including cued movements in sequences can also increase motivation.

SESSION 4 ACTIONS

SESSION 4:1 BACK FOUR ("BACK FOUR")

What you will need:
• Clicker
• 40 treats
• Yoga space
• Two pots (active and non-active)

1. Count out ten treats and hold one in your hand.
2. Ask your dog to "stand".
3. Hold the hand with the treat in it under your dog's chin.
4. Click and treat his step back when he steps back to get the treat (you can treat from the hand you are holding the treat in on this occasion).
5. Repeat, but this time hold the click and treat back until two steps have been taken backwards.
6. Repeat, but now hold the click treat back for four steps.
7. Repeat asking for four steps until there are no treats left in your active pot.

8. Count out ten more treats into the pot and have one ready in your hand.
9. Ask your dog to "stand".
10. Hold the hand (without the treat in it) slightly back but below your dog's nose height and say "back four" and wait...
11. Click and treat any backwards motion.
12. Repeat until there are no treats left in your active pot, each time reducing the hand motion and saying "back four" clearly...remember to be patient!
13. Take a well-deserved break.
14. Count out ten more treats.
15. Now point backwards to the dog from situ and say "back four" and wait...
17. Click any steps backwards and treat.
18. Repeat this until you have run out of active treats, but each time hold the clicker back to get four steps.
19. Count out ten treats.
20. Ask your dog to "stand".
21. Ask for "back four".
22. Click and treat.
23. Repeat until there are no treats left.

Yey! You have completed your first action! That is really exciting and you definitely need to celebrate. Think up a way to ensure your dog gets the party he deserves for learning all this hard stuff!

SESSION 4:2: FORWARD FOUR ("FOR FOUR")

What you will need:
• Clicker
• 40 treats
• Yoga space
• Two pots (one active and one passive)

Back four.

1. Count out ten treats and have one in your hand ready.
2. Ask your dog to "back four".
3. Ask your dog to "come".
4. Click as soon as he has started moving forward and immediately (before you treat) ask him to "stand".
5. Treat. I'm sure some purist clicker trainers will have something to say about clicking a dog for moving forward, then asking for something else before he receives the treat, but I think in this context it makes learning this action easier for the dog.

Forward four.

6. Repeat this until you run out of treats in your active pot.
7. Now count out ten more treats.
8. Ask your dog to "back four".
9. Now instead of the recall command say "for four".
10. Wait until your dog starts moving toward you.
11. After four paces, put a stop sign out with your hand (palm facing dog) but don't use the verbal command.
12. Click his stop (even if it is after more than four paces).
13. Treat.
14. Repeat until there are no more treats in the active pot.
15. Take a break.
16. Count out ten more treats.

17. Ask your dog to "back four".
18. Ask for "for four"...wait...this time no stop signs – just wait for the stop.
19. Click and treat any pausing or stopping.
20. Now repeat this shaping for four steps.
21. Count our your final ten treats.
22. Ask for a "down".
23. Ask for a "stand".
24. Ask for "for four".
25. Click and treat the four steps and the stop.
26. Ask for a "back four".
27. Click and treat.
28. Ask for "for four".
29. Click and treat the four steps and the stop.
30. Repeat until there are no treats left.

You have finished your stepping actions! I bet they weren't as hard as you thought? Right, cuddles and games for the pooch now. He deserves them!

SESSION 4:3: LEFT SPIN ("LEFT SPIN")

What you will need:
• Clicker
• Treats
• Yoga space
• Two pots (active and-non active)

1. Count out ten treats.
2. Ask for "stretch left".
3. Hold off the click and treat until one foot moves to the left.
4. Repeat, shaping the left until your dog begins to turn.
5. Count out ten treats.
6. Don't ask for the "stretch left" this time, just wait for him to guess that it is now left motions that get him the click.

Left spin.

7. Keep shaping this up, increasing your criteria in small increments.
8. Wait for him to complete a circle himself.
9. Click and treat at the end of the circle.
10. Count out ten more treats.
11. Continue the process of shaping until he is frequently performing full circles.
12. Now begin saying "spin left" just before you point.
13. Click and treat the spin.

All done – again, not too hard. The motion training in many ways is easier than the posture training as its more what we are used to. Good job though, pat on the back for you and a cuddle for your dog

SESSION 4:4: RIGHT SPIN ("RIGHT SPIN")

Repeat the method above but, this time, do it in the other direction. If you or your dog struggle with shaping the spin, you can lure it instead. Below are instructions to teach the right spin via luring if you prefer.

What you will need:
• Clicker
• 40 treats
• Yoga space
• Two pots (active and non-active)

1. Count out ten treats.
2. Lure your dog in a circle right.
3. Click and treat on the halfway point.
4. Repeat this until you have no active treats left.
5. Now begin only luring half the circle and breaking your hand in suddenly so that the dog completes the rest of the circle without the hand lure...

6. Count out ten treats.
7. Move your hand in a short semi-circle to lure your dog half way round to the right.
8. Wait for him to complete the circle himself.
9. Click and treat at the end of the circle.
10. Repeat this, giving less and less of a hand lure each time.
11. Count out ten more treats.
12. Continue the process of fading the lure so that your dog will spin right from the cue of the hand pointing right.
13. Now begin saying "spin right" just before you point.
14. Click and treat the "spin right".
15. Count out ten more treats.
16. Ask your dog to "spin left".
17. Click and treat.
18. Ask your dog to "spin right".
19. Click and treat.

All done on the spin front. I love these actions as they are great fun to practise out and about as well.

Right spin.

As we can see, we use an object to begin teaching the circle left. As opposed to the spins, the circles expect moderate movement and control which generates more distance. That means the circles should be wide and require the dog to pace, whereas the spins should happen on the spot

SESSION 4:5: LEFT CIRCLE TURN ("CIRCLE LEFT")

What you will need

Clicker

• 60 treats

• Yoga space

• Two pots (active and non-active)

• A cone, chair or large bottle, or a similar object

1. Count out ten treats.
2. Again, shaping is possible and can be fun to do if you feel like it. However, luring seems to make more sense to the dog, so take a treat in your hand to use as a lure.
3. Stand by your cone/object and, using your lure hand (the hand with the treat), lead the dog in a full circle round the object.
4. Click half way round and treat at the end.
5. Repeat this nine more times.
6. Now count out ten further treats.
7. Start fading the lure hand, just luring the dog part way round the cone. Click when he chooses to take the rest of the steps around the cone, and treat when the circle is complete.
8. Click when your dog independently starts to take steps towards the treat hand around the cone/object without the lure.
9. Repeat this, each time using less and less of a hand lure so that the dog is moving around the cone by himself.
10. Count a further ten treats.
11. Point to the left of the cone and say "circle left"...wait.
12. Click and treat the full circle round.
13. Repeat until there are no treats left.
14. Take a well earned break.
15. Before asking your dog to return to the space, remove the cone/object and exchange it for something small and flat like a coaster or a magazine.
16. Count out ten treats.
17. Ask your dog to "circle left" pointing left of the new object and wait...
18. Click and treat the circle round. If he really struggles use a tiny hint of a lure again but be patient – allow him time to work it out
19. When you point, remember to point to the

far left so that it is a 45 degree angle to your dog. You don't want him to think of spinning and ideally you will shape him (so only click the best ones) so that he walks right round the smaller object and not too close to it.

20. Count out ten more treats.
21. Now remove the object and use a small piece of paper.
22. Repeat the above asking for "circle left"
23. Click and treat those large circles around the object.
24. Now count out ten more treats.
25. Repeat the above but each time your dog goes around the paper, tear it in half until there is no paper left.

Phew! You guys deserve a break and a game or a run, so throw caution to the wind and get some air! The circles are quite hard to learn so be really appreciative of your dog's progress and, remember, it doesn't really matter if a posture, action or expression takes more than one session to learn.

SESSION 4:6: RIGHT CIRCLE TURN ("CIRCLE RIGHT")

What you will need:
- Clicker
- 70 treats
- Yoga space
- Two pots (active and non-active)
- The objects you used last time

1. Count out ten treats and hold a treat in your hand to use as a lure.
2. Stand by your largest cone object and, using your lure, lead the dog in a full circle right, round the object (as you did above).

3. Click half way round and treat at the end.
4. Repeat this nine more times.
5. Now count out ten further treats.
6. This time, lure the dog half way round the cone object and then hold your hand the other side to encourage him to move right round the cone and then to accept the treat.
7. Repeat this, each time using less and less of an initial hand lure so that the dog is moving around the cone by himself as above.
8. Count a further ten treats.
9. Point to the right of the cone and say "circle right"...wait.
10. Click and treat the full circle right round.
11. Repeat until there are no treats left.
12. Take a well-earned break.
13. Before asking your dog to return to the space, remove the cone object and exchange it for something small, and flat, such as a coaster or a magazine.
14. Count out ten treats.

Circle right

15. Ask your dog to "circle right" pointing right of the new object and wait...
16. Click and treat the circle round. If he really struggles use a tiny hint of a lure but be patient – allow him time to work it out.
17. Count out ten more treats.
18. Now remove the object and use a small piece of paper.
19. Repeat the above asking for "circle right" and pointing.
20. Click and treat those large circles, right turn, around the object.
21. Now count out ten more treats.
22. Ask for "circle right".
23. Repeat the above but each time your dog goes around the paper, tear it in half until there is no paper left.
24. Count out ten more treats.
25. Ask for a "circle left".
26. Click and treat.
27. Ask for a "circle right".
28. Click and treat.
29. Repeat until there are no treats left.

Now reward your dog with a good cuddle and a few rounds of hide and seek with a toy.

SESSION 4:7: HEAD SHAKE ("SAY NO")

What you will need:
• Clicker
• 40 treats
• Yoga space
• Two pots (active and non-active)

1. Count out ten treats.
2. Begin by practising a sequence of "stretch left" followed immediately by "stretch right".
3. Count out ten more treats.
4. Now remove the verbal cue and just use your head nods to infer that you would like the "stretch left" then "stretch right".
5. Repeat a couple of times, clicking each change of direction.
6. Count out five treats.
7. Use a slow shaking head cue and wait. This should infer you would like a "stretch left" and then a "stretch right". Wait and don't click until you have a left and then right head shake.
8. Repeat this.
9. Count out five more treats.

Say no.

10. Shake your head, but this time you are going to wait until you get a left-right then another left-right. So that is two shakes from one cue.
11. Count out ten treats.
12. Say "say no" and do a head shake clearly and slowly.
13. Click once your dog has looked first left and then right, and then left then right.
14. Repeat this and begin to play around with how many "stretch lefts" and "stretch rights" you click on.
15. Take a break.
16. When you return, count out your last ten treats.
17. Ask for "say no" and shake your head... wait.
18. Click and treat the head shake.
19. Repeat until you are out of treats.

Head shakes are not too hard. You are getting to a point where your dog's vocabulary is so good that you can explain what you want with prior knowledge. That's a great place to be, but make sure you give him a good cuddle tonight because there are some hard ones ahead!

SESSION 4:8: FULL BODY SHAKE OFF ("SHAKE OFF")

The body shake is one of the hardest actions to teach your dog. Broadly speaking, a dog uses the shake-off to convey two things. First, he uses it to show that he is moving away from an excited or anxious state and into a thinking state, i.e. he is coming down into a lower adrenaline state. Secondly dogs use it to shake off when they are wet or muddy!

When used socially, this behaviour marks that the dog is communicating to the other dog that he is moving toward neutrality. He wants predictability and security from the situation – he does not want a confrontation.

More often than not, shake-offs are seen when a dog is either wet or out and about. This is when potential environmental or social stressors are likely. Take it on board and make a note of when your dog is shaking as it implies (unless he is wet), that there has been something that has caused his level of arousal to increase and that he is now coming back down.

Putting a "shake off" on cue is really tricky for the following reason. Dogs naturally shake when something stresses them out, and we know that stress reduces a dog's capability to learn (and is unpleasant). However, there are certain situations when a dog is very likely to shake – when he comes out from a bath or a swim, for example, and when he walks away from a polite social introduction. These are environmental predictors of the behaviour and don't cause unpleasant stress – so let's use them!

If your dog is capable of polite and easy-going meet and greets with other dogs
If your dog is a socially chilled kind of creature who finds meeting and greeting fun and easy, then take him to the dog park on lead. Take him over to meet and greet another dog and wait for him to shake off after the encounter.

Click and treat the shake-off, then repeat. You can set this up with other dog friends.

If you use this technique, it is really important that your dog is not frustrated, over-excited or anxious around other dogs. Dogs in that state are unable to learn. Keep clicking and treating the shake-offs as many times as you can. What we are hoping to see is an increase in shake-offs. Once there is a noticeable increase, begin to ask for "shake-off" when you see your dog beginning to shake-off. If you feel that your dog is beginning to shake-off more consciously, on cue, then ramp up the reinforcement. This means lots of praise, movement and happy cuddles as well as treats after the click.

If the shake-off becomes reliable, begin to move out of this context and ask for it. It is highly likely that your dog will shake-off when he comes home anyway. So when you get home and he does shake-off, click it and treat it and continue training it. Once it is on cue, and reliably so, then ask him into the Yoga space to practise it among other postures and actions.

If your dog is not capable of polite and easy-going meet and greets with other dogs, but he likes water...

Again, this is such a difficult balance to get right. If your dog is too excited by water, or if he doesn't like water, this method is not advisable. If, however, he is a fan of water and doesn't find it too arousing then by all means...

1. Count out ten treats.
2. Get a bit of tissue and soak it.
3. Say "shake-off" to predict dripping a little drop of water over your dog's head.
4. Click any level of shake (even just the beginnings of a shake with his head) and treat.
5. Repeat this for ten treats.
6. Count out ten more treats.

Full body shake-off (if your dog likes water).

7. Now say "shake-off" and drip a little drop of water, but wait it out until you get a full body shake (which you will get if you wait) before you click and treat.
8. Repeat this for nine more treats.
9. Count out ten more treats.
10. Ask for the "shake-off".
11. Now use dry tissue and pretend to drip the water.
12. Wait for the shake off – be patient!
13. Click and treat.
14. Repeat.

If your dog is not capable of polite and easy meet and greets, and doesn't like water, try this...
The third way to teach it is tricky but it can be done – have faith!

1. Count out ten treats in your hand.
2. Walk out of the door leaving your dog in the room for 30 seconds.
3. Walk in the room and greet your dog happily.
4. Wait for a shake.
5. Click and treat.
6. Repeat ten times.
7. Repeat the above, but start predicting the shake-off when you see that it is likely by saying "shake off".
8. Count out ten more treats.
9. What you are looking for, as above, is an increase in frequency.
10. Repeat the steps, but this time do not actually leave the room.
11. Approach the door, turn around, go back to your dog and greet him.
12. Wait and predict the shake-off by asking for it verbally – "shake off".
13. Click and treat.

14. Count out ten more treats.
15. Go to the door, turn back to your dog and greet him.
16. Now ask for the "shake-off" and wait.
17. Click and treat the shake-off.
18. Repeat until you have no treats left.
19. This time, count out ten treats.
20. Ask for the "shake-off" without going to the door.
21. Wait and click and treat the shake-off.
22. Repeat until you are out of treats.

This method of using the environment and context to prompt a behaviour, and then capture it, is very different from the methods outlined above and it is unlikely that this action can be trained in one session. Stick with it, though, and do not beat yourself up when it doesn't always go exactly as you would like or you would expect.

SESSION 4:9: BOW ("BOW")
Dogs use bows in play to communicate that they are looking to have some fun! A dog will also bow when he is getting ready to run and chase something or when he is greeting a loved one. Putting this friendly and social behaviour on cue is great for impulse control. Dogs naturally become a little aroused from this action so by providing a training context for it and controlling the bow, we can teach our dogs to control their excited impulses.

What you will need:
• Clicker
• 30 treats
• Yoga space
• Two pots (active and non-active)

1. For slightly excitable dogs who bow regularly in play we can capture this behaviour.
2. Count out ten treats and be ready with your clicker
3. Make a little "woof" noise, get on your hands and knees and pat the floor with your hands in a playful, staccato motion.
4. This usually brings a bow out in dogs who play bow a lot in natural behaviour.
5. Capture the bow with a click and reward.
6. Go again until you have captured ten bows.
7. Repeat the process above but stop "woofing" and begin, instead saying "bow" as you pat the floor with your hands palms down.
8. Repeat the process again but this time, instead of patting the floor, stand or sit in situ and pat the air (as if playing an imaginary air organ) as you ask for the bow.
9. Click and treat the bows.
10. Begin shaping them so only click the most obvious bows.

If your dog is not a bower...

1. Count out ten treats and have one in your hand ready to use.
2. With a treat in your hand, lure your dog down into a bow position.
3. Click and treat. To begin with the bow may look more like a lean down, but that is OK. We can shape it to get it right.
4. Keep clicking and treating a half-down position and begin to fade your lure hand.
5. Start asking for "bow" and signalling to your dog without a food lure.
6. Keep fading the hand and asking until you can prompt the posture from your normal situ without any lure at all.

Bows are always fun – they look cool too! You and Fido are now well on your way to becoming real Dog Yoginis! Waggy tails, smiles and cuddles all round.

Bow.

PAW TARGETS

Paw targets are fantastic for teaching careful, slow, disciplined movements. Dogs tend to take their weight off the front paws (in motions like paw lifts) to put the weight in their hindquarters when they are ready to run or react suddenly. When a dog moves his weight on to his back, it is usually in preparation of movement so we watch for this as an anticipatory sign which implies a dog is perhaps feeling uneasy. Whether this is anticipating a pounce, a game, or because he is worried and anticipating flight or a fight, it is useful to be able to spot this weight shift. Teaching a dog careful and considered paw movements helps him to control this weight shift and helps us to learn to spot it more easily. It is great for sporting dogs, too as it practises flexibility and increases body consciousness, focus and accuracy.

SESSION 4:10: FRONT RIGHT PAW TARGET ("TARGET RIGHT")

What you will need:
- Clicker
- 40 treats
- Two pots (one with treats in, one without)
- A circular piece of paper and scissors

1. Count out 20 treats into the active pot and have one in your hand ready. This one is a matter of repetition so be ready for quick and accurate clicks.
2. Place the paper on the floor.
3. Wait and click and treat every time your dog's front paw (right) touches the paper.
4. Repeat this again and again until your dog works out that it is the right, front paw touching the target that is earning the treat. We are looking for definite and obvious movements and an increase in frequency.
5. Count out ten more treats and begin to ask for "target right" and point at the target.
6. Take a break using the usual protocol.
7. Count out a further ten treats.
8. Ask for "target right".
9. Click and treat.

Hurray, all done! That's a tricky one so you might want to really dedicate some time, after you have taught the other paws, to practising this

and making it really accurate. Well done on the first one! Now spent 10 minutes on lots of cuddles and games!

SESSION 4:11 FRONT LEFT PAW TARGET ("TARGET LEFT")

You will need:
- Clicker
- 55 treats
- Yoga space
- Two pots (one active, one passive)

Repeat the whole process above, but this time with the left front paw instead. Remember that dogs have a paw bias and so one paw might be significantly easier than the other. That said, after doing the paw lifts and other paw actions and postures, hopefully your dog won't find it too tricky.

Front right paw target.

Once you have the "target left", then count
out 15 treats and practise "target right" and
"target left" so that it is clear your dog can
differentiate between the two commands
easily.

A game with your dog and a rest is needed!
Tomorrow we will work on the back legs. This
will be a new concept and may be difficult for
your dog...

BACK FOOT TARGETING

Back foot targeting is tricky! It is not easy as
we never usually ask our dogs to use their
back feet in this manner. It is, however, very
good for your dog for many reasons. It not only
improves accuracy and focus, but also plays
with the dog's concept of weight. As suggested
before, a dog usually shifts his weight forward
when he is more confident, investigating
something or playing. Teaching him actions
which move weight forward consciously
can improve confidence as well as enhance
control. For competition dogs this can be great
in terms of enhancing control for skills such
as weaving as well.

SESSION 4:12 BACK RIGHT PAW TARGET ("STICKER RIGHT")

What you will need:
• Clicker
• 60 treats
• Two pots (one active with no treats in and
  one non-active)
• A piece of paper
• Yoga space

1. Count out 20 treats and hold one in your
   hand.
2. Put the paper on the ground.
3. Lure your dog forward so that his back foot
   hits the paper.
4. Click and treat the contact on the target.
5. Repeat this and start slowly fading the lure.
6. Count out ten more treats.
7. Ask for "sticker left".
8. If you need to lure a little, that's fine.
   However, the aim is to start fading the lure.
9. Click and treat the back foot contact.
10. Take a break with the usual protocol.
11. Count out ten more treats.
12. Ask for a "sticker right"...wait...
13. Click and treat that back contact. If your
    dog struggles, repeat the whole of the
    above again.
14. Now count out another ten treats.
15. Ask for the "sticker right".
16. Repeat.

Loads of cuddling, please. Lots of fuss and do
something which allows your dog to release
tension and let off steam. This session is
intense and hard!

SESSION 4: 13 BACK LEFT PAW TARGET ("STICKER LEFT")

Teach the other back paw target exactly as you
have the first. If you know your dog struggles
with one left or right paw, as noted earlier, it is
worth starting with the easier paw to teach the
initial action.

Once the other back paw target is achieved
then count out 20 treats and have some fun

asking for the various paw targets. Ensure your dog is completely aware of the various commands. Keep praise high and make sure you are rewarding with clicks and treats, too.

What you and your dog have achieved is fantastic. It is brilliant that he is able to control his body to this degree and that he is so connected to you. The learning process you have joined one another on is a beautiful journey.

Back left paw on target.

SESSION 4: 14: ALL FOUR FEET ON TARGETS ("ALL FOURS")

What you need:
• Clicker
• 50 treats
• Two pots
• Four paper targets
   stuck to the floor in position
• Yoga space

1. Count out ten treats.
2. Ask for "sticker left" (or "right" if your dog has a right hand bias).
3. Do not click and treat, instead ask for "target left".
4. Click and treat if your dog keeps his back left target and gets the right target, too.
5. Repeat nine more times.
6. Count out ten more treats.
7. Repeat above, but this time when you get the two paw targets, ask for another front paw target.
8. Click and treat when you get all three targets.

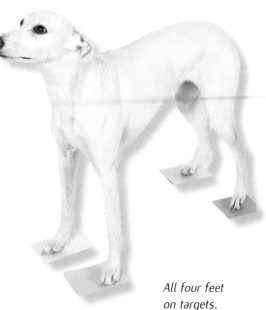

All four feet on targets.

9. Repeat for nine more treats.

10. Count out ten more treats.

11. Ask for the "sticker left", then 'left target", then "right target". Before you click and treat, ask for "sticker right'.

12. Repeat this and toss the treat on the floor so that each time you are starting again.

13. Count out ten treats.

14. Ask for "all fours".

15. Wait patiently for your dog to adjust his posture on to the paw targets. If he is struggling, use hand points to help him out and, as your repeat it, begin fading the hand motions.

16. Take a break with the usual protocol.

17. Count out your final ten treats.

18. Ask for "all fours".

19. Click and treat the action.

20. Repeat until you're out of treats.

Well done! You have done all your foot target commands. Treats, cuddles and play is definitely in order.

SESSION 4:15 NOSE TARGET TOUCH ("TARGET")

Sniffing the floor is an action dogs do for lots of reasons and with some important consequences. Obviously a dog will sniff the floor to investigate scent information. He will also use sniffing as a negotiation tool. For example, if he wishes to cross into the path of another dog, or if he wants come closer to something that may be valuable to another dog or creature. The sniff in this context is polite and means: "I don't want any trouble, I just want to move to this area. Is that acceptable?" The dog suggests: He would like to move in, but he's going to test the water because he really doesn't want any trouble.

A dog will also use sniffing as a displacement behaviour – for example, if he is anxious or stressed about a potential conflict and wants to appease the situation and avoid conflict. It is a bit like seeing a spider (if you are scared of spiders) and deciding to do the washing up to take your mind off it.

Nose targets.

What you will need:
- Clicker
- 50 treats
- Two pots (active and non-active as usual)
- A piece of paper taped to the floor
- Yoga space

1. Count out ten treats.
2. Put a treat on the target.
3. As your dog touches to take the treat, click and feed another treat by hand.
4. Repeat this five times.
5. Now count out ten more treats.
6. Wait for your dog to sniff the target again.
7. Click and treat and praise as soon as he does.
8. Repeat.
9. Count out ten more treats.
10. Ask for "nose target" and point at the target.
11. Click, treat and repeat until there are no more treats left in the active pot.
12. Take a break.
13. Remove the paper.
14. Count out ten treats.
15. Ask for the "nose target" and point.
16. Click and treat.
17. If your dog seems to have got this one (it's pretty easy really) then...
18. Count out the remaining treats and ask for paw targets and mix them in with the nose target, too. Make it fun and exciting by tossing treats as opposed to feeding them by hand.

Actions complete! You are a genius, and so is your dog – you should be super proud of each other. Reward each other by playing some awesome, fun games.

SESSION 5
EXPRESSIONS

Some owners I meet think they can read their dogs' faces, and others find it nearly impossible to see and interpret their dogs' expressions. Your dog is talking to you all the time using his face, we just need to learn to watch and acknowledge this. The following expressions are used in dog communication. It is encouraging, challenging and smart to teach a dog to give these expressions on cue as it helps with impulse control, focus and a more conscious communication with other dogs and other creatures. It is great for people to learn to observe these expressions more clearly, too.

SESSION 5:1 NOSE LICK ("LICK LICK")

Dogs use tongue flicking as a negotiation tool, usually a gesture of polite but slightly escalated conflict avoidance, and as a warning signal when something is causing them stress. Warning signals and passive gestures, such as tongue movements, ear movements, eye orientation, etc. should be encouraged and noted. An action, such as nose/lip lick is a dog speaking, expressing concern. Seldom, as everyday dog owners, do we note or respond to this kind of facial signalling. Once we have put it on cue we are more conscious of the expression and, thus, more likely to recognise it being used in the future in natural practice.

If we reinforce something (as we are in this training), it is more likely to be used in everyday natural behaviour. So by reinforcing these more passive gestures and expressions, we are helping to expand a dog's polite vocabulary. We are encouraging him to say: "excuse me, would you be so kind as to offer me a little space", rather than pushing him to swear, shout and scream to communicate his message.

What you will need:
• Clicker
• 30 treats
• Two pots (one with treats, one without)
• Yoga space

Nose lick.

1. Count out ten treats.
2. Hold a treat between your fingers and allow your dog to sniff it.
3. Hold the treat up and wait.
4. Click as soon as he licks his lips. Waiting is the hard part here as, to begin with, your dog is likely to give you his entire repertoire. If he gets aroused and frustrated, ask him into a "sit" (or go into his comfortable default posture – for sighthounds and collie-types this might be a "down") and continue waiting.
5. Click and treat those lip licks. Owners are often surprised at how quickly dogs learn this but, in fact, it is a very easy to learn as we are simply rewarding a natural behaviour. The key with this expression (and all the expressions), is extinction of the expression being frequently given without the verbal cue. We have to stop the dog continually licking his lips and teach him that in the training context, we will only reward expressions when they have been asked for. This means we must focus on only rewarding the expressions when they have been verbally cued.
6. Take a short break.
7. Count out ten more treats.
8. Ask for the "lick lick".
9. Wait and then click and treat him when he does it.
10. Now wait a few seconds, ignoring the lip licks when he offers them off cue (without you asking).
11. Ask again for the "lick lick" and click and treat it.
12. Now ask for a "down", a "settle", a "target left" and a "stretch right", clicking and treating each command.

13. Now ask for a "lick lick" again – click and treat it.
14. Repeat the above, mixing the "lick lick" with other postures and actions to ensure he understands the verbal cue.

Awesome – first expression complete. Isn't it amazing how much you and your dog have learnt since starting this training? Dogs are so much smarter than we give them credit for, but now you can see just how smart your dog is! Lots of praise and cuddles, and treat yourself, too – you are doing a great job.

SESSION 5:2: YAWN ("OPEN WIDE")

Essentially creatures yawn to increase the oxygen to the brain. Dogs yawn when they are tired, but also when they are a little stressed. The body language which comes with the yawn is the best clue as to whether your dog is yawning as a result of tiredness, or yawning as a result of stress. Whether it is intentional or not, we will never know, but the yawn has also become a negotiation strategy in social situations. A dog interprets another dog's yawn as a sign of not wanting conflict. It is commonplace to see this being mirrored, although it may just be that these yawns are contagious, as they are for humans!

Teaching an expression, such as a yawn, is useful for many reasons. One, of course being that teaching an open mouth on cue is extremely handy for teeth checking and cleaning, and for medicating. It is also a way of pulling the dog 'back in the room' – helping him to come back from a stressful situation.

What you will need:
- Clicker
- Patience
- 60 treats
- Yoga space

1. Wait in the Yoga space until your dog yawns, opens his mouth or begins to vocalise. Whilst this sounds crazy, if you wait it out, one of these three things will happen. You must have faith but, essentially, if you don't ask for anything and sit in the training space, your dog is likely to feel a little confusion, which causes the yawn to occur. Some more confident dogs do not experience this confusion and simply get frustrated. This causes vocalisations, which also lead to an open mouth.

Yawn.

101

For this expression we don't worry about whether we are training an actual yawn, or whether we are just cueing the dog to open his mouth. If neither of these responses happen, your dog is likely to lip lick as this was the last thing he was taught. So click at the very beginning as soon as your dog opens his mouth.

2. Repeat the above and if you are using slightly frustrated vocalising, ensure that you are clicking at the very beginning before the loudest part of the noise. You want to be really accurate here so that it is clear to the dog that it is the open mouth that gets a click. Even try clicking just before you think the vocalising is coming, as it will stop your dog from thinking that you are asking him to bark at you. If you are using the "lick lick", try to shape the open mouth by holding off the click when the tongue comes out, and clicking again next time he offers at the start.

3. We train the expressions last as handlers are more natural with the clicker by now. This level of accuracy and careful shaping would not have been possible at the start of this journey but, hopefully, you are now used to using the clicker in this way, and have grown good at responding on time to your dog. Keep shaping, and remember to lower your criteria if you are not clicking very much.

4. Repeat this until the open mouth increases in frequency.

5. Now count out more treats and begin only clicking the wider open mouth expressions.

6. Again, make sure that you are keeping your criteria low enough so that it is easy for the dog.

7. Repeat until you are getting frequent, open mouth expressions.

8. Take a break.

9. Now count out ten more treats.

10. Start using a cue, saying "open wide", then clicking and treating the open mouth.

11. Repeat until you are confident and then start shaping out any unwanted behaviour which you may have accidentally trained. This means only clicking minimal vocalisation and then no vocalisation, a just opened mouth (silent), or only clicking minimal lip licks and then none.

12. Now count out ten more treats.

13. Ask for a "lick lick".

14. Click and treat.

15. Ask for "open wide".

16. Click and treat.

17. Repeat until you are out of treats.

Lots of pats on the back for you! For some reason this one is always much harder for the handler than for the dog. This means you deserve extra chocolate and cuddles with your dog!

SESSION 5:3: SIGH ("BORED")

Dogs sigh as a sign of boredom or acceptance, but also as a way of cooling down when they are tired and/or hot. Putting a sigh on cue can really help you to encourage your dog to chill out and settle when you need him to. By asking for a "settle left' or "settle right", then asking for the "bored", you are providing a context and making it very clear that you want your dog to chill.

What you will need:
- Clicker
- 60 treats
- Yoga space
- Yoga mat or dog bed
- A non-active and an active pot

1. Count out ten treats.
2. Ask your dog to "settle left" or "right" (whichever is most comfortable).
3. Wait and wait...if he breaks the settle, ask him to "settle" again.
4. When he sighs, or gives a hard, outwards breath, capture this with a click.
5. Toss a treat on the floor.
6. Repeat until you have no treats left in your active pot.
7. Count out ten treats.
8. Wait for the sigh without asking for the "settle left" or "right" this time.
9. Capture it with a click and treat.
10. Repeat until there are no treats left in the active pot.
11. Now count out a further ten treats.
12. Ask for "bored" and wait for the sigh.
13. Click, treat and repeat.
14. Take a break with all the usual protocols.
15. Count out 20 remaining treats.
16. Ask for "bored"
17. Click and treat.
18. Ask for "open wide".
19. Click and treat.
20. Ask for "bored".
21. Click and treat.
22. Repeat the above until you have no treats left.

Well done! These mouth expressions are hard because we need patience and faith that the expression will come. We are not used to dealing with dogs' mouths, or putting mouth movements or expressions on cue. But when you think about it, for the dog, it is no different to asking for a "paw "or a "sit!" You are all doing so well – a fun game is on the cards I should think!

SESSION 5:4 SMILE ("SMILE")

Dogs, like people, often smile. Not all dogs smile and some owners will have to skip this expression. Smiling and snarling is very different, and it is really important that you can tell the two apart!

Sigh.

When dogs are super excited and glad to see you, they may pull their lips back in a happy show of teeth. This is combined with a soft expression and relaxed body, where the movement and weight is moving forward, and is an excitable and usually very happy posture. Teaching a dog (who naturally smiles) to smile on cue is great for teaching impulse control, and teaching self-control. Arousal usually shoots up when a smile is shown, so teaching a dog to exhibit excitable facial expressions and to keep control is a really great if tricky process!

What you will need:
• Clicker
• 50 treats
• Yoga space

1. Count out 15 treats.
2. Get a treat in your hand and gee-up your dog. It may be that there are certain scenarios where your dog exhibits the smile expression naturally. If this is the case, set up these scenarios (e.g. pretend to go out and return).

3. As with the other expressions we are capturing, then shaping. This makes it harder to be organised with precisely how the training will go. It means that you need to be flexible, trusting and patient. Make sure you are particularly calm, forgiving and focused when you start training these expressions.
4. Click the smile and say "good smile".
5. While he is in this emotional state, you may get three or four smiles so continue to keep happy-talk up and move around.
6. Once you have managed to illicit, capture and reward 15 smiles...
7. Count out ten treats.
8. Ask for "smile".
9. Wait...
10. Be patient, allow for a little frustration but not too much. Using a moving hand gesture, such as wiggling the fingers on one hand, may help to remind your dog that he was feeling excited when he was being clicked previously.
11. Click and treat the smile, but if you are not getting it, repeat the steps above and then try again.
12. Take a break once you have got ten cued smiles, or if you are finding yourself feeling frustrated.
13. Return and count out 15 treats.
14. Ask for a "lip lick".
15. Click and treat.
16. Ask for a "smile".
17. Click and treat.
18. Ask for a "bored".
19. Click and treat.

Smile.

20. Ask for an "open wide".
21. Click and treat.
22. Ask for a "smile".
23. Click and treat.
24. Repeat until there are no treats left.

Are you finding these tricky? Is your dog still enjoying the training? It's so important that you are still having fun. If not, go back and run through some of the older exercises for the next few days. Keep criteria low and reward frequently, then return to these expressions when your feeling more inspired. It has to be enjoyable because training is on-going.

SESSION 5:5: SLOW BLINKING ("BLINKY")

Soft blinking is good. It is a negotiation signal. A dog that has his eyes closed is usually either asleep or suggesting that he is passive and friendly. Teaching dogs to close their eyes helps prompt a natural state of relaxation. But, please, never ask your dog to fake a closed eye or any of the blinking expressions when he is in a stressful, potentially stressful, or social situation.

What you will need:
• Clicker
• 35 treats
• Two pots (non-active and active)
• Yoga space

1. Count out ten treats.
2. Close your eyes in a soft blink at your dog, and wait for him to return it.
3. Click and treat as soon as he closes his eyes or one eye.

4. Repeat this ten times.
5. Count out ten more treats.
6. Say "blinky".
7. Close your eyes.
8. Wait for him to close his eyes or one eye.
9. Click and treat.
10. Repeat until there are no treats left in your active pot.
11. Take a break with the usual protocols.
12. Count out 15 more treats.
13. Ask for "blinky" then instead of clicking and treating, ask again.
14. Now click and treat.
15. Ask for "blinky" after the dog has blinked. Wait until he blinks a few more times before you click and treat.
16. Continue and repeat so that your dog is repeating the blink until he hears the click.

Hurray – we love soft blinks! Cuddles and a walk or a game should be your dog's reward for all the hard work he has put in.

Slow blinking.

SESSION 5:6: CLOSE EYES ("SLEEP")

What you will need:

• Clicker
• 40 treats
• Two pots (non-active and active)
• Yoga space

1. Count out 25 treats.
2. Ask for "blinky".
3. You are now going to wait and shape, so only click longer blinks.
4. This is quite technical so be really vigilant and accurate. You may want to count in your head so that you know how long the blinks last for.
5. Repeat until there are no treats left.
6. Count out 15 more treats.
7. Repeat the process above, but start holding off the click when your dog opens his eyes. This might mean that your dog does two long blinks, which is fine.
8. Repeat, but only click the longest blinks.

9. Begin shaping so that means only clicking the blinks of longer and then longer duration.
10. Continue and repeat until your dog is waiting for the click to open his eyes.
11. Take a break with the usual protocols.
12. Repeat the above, but this time start saying "sleep" and then clicking those long blinks.

These eye expressions are great! If you have a dog with particularly hard eyes, such as Collie types and Vizslas, begin to shape in softness as well. Start giving extra treats for soft, happy eyes and holding off clicking fixated stares.

EAR EXPRESSIONS

Ear expressions tell us a lot about the seriousness of a situation. When the ears are forced forward there is usually a lot of intent behind them, albeit to chase, to investigate or maybe to run away. When the ears are relaxed, the situation is usually less intense. When they are held back or firmly back this usually indicates your dog is 'on his back foot', i.e. that he is thinking that the situation may become, or is, a little stressful or unpredictable. Watch your dog's ears and see how he uses them to show his mood in every given situation. Ear twitching in situations when dogs are thinking and processing, are sometimes used as a way to diffuse tension. Improving muscle control in the ears helps dogs to communicate more consciously and helps us to learn to really notice those ears.

Close eyes.

SESSION 5:7: EAR PRICK ("IS IT?")

What you need:
- Clicker
- 30 treats
- A non-active and an active pot
- Yoga space

1. Count out ten treats.
2. Ask your dog "is it?" in an excited voice.
3. Click and treat the ear prick (which should come as a result of the elevated tone of the "is it?" command).
4. Your timing has to be good, so be vigilant.
5. Repeat ten times.
6. Count out ten more treats.
7. It sounds backwards, but wait and stop using the verbal cue.
8. Just click and treat the ears moving forward for ten clicks. We are doing this for clarity and to make it super clear that it's not the increase of arousal or the onset of excitement we are rewarding, but the ear movement.
9. Count ten treats ready in your active pot and then take the usual break.
10. On your return ask "is it?" Try to keep your tone neutral - especially if your dog does suffer from high arousal.
11. Click and treat the ear movements forward.
12. Repeat this for nine more treats.

The ear prick is pretty easy, but make sure you feel that your dog has really 'got it'. The idea is to reduce the energy behind it, so it is important we are not just putting excitement on cue here. Pat on the back and praise all round, followed by a game of hide and seek!

Ear expressions communicate a lot of information.

SESSION 5:8 EARS BACK ("IT'S NOT")

What you will need:
- Clicker
- 40 treats
- Your two pots

1. Count out ten treats into the active pot with one in your hand ready to use.
2. Because you were doing ear pricks yesterday, it is quite likely that your dog will instantly come over and take a sit with his ears pricked ready. This is great as it gives you a chance to wait until they go back.
3. Simply wait until the ears 'unprick'. They don't need to go properly back just yet – relaxed or slightly less alert is fine to start with.
4. Click and treat backwards ear motions until you run out of treats.
5. If your dog's backwards ear motions are not increasing in frequency, duration or intensity, count out ten more treats and keep going.
6. Count out a further ten treats.
7. Ask for "it's not" and wait for the ears to move back.
8. Click and treat, then repeat.

9. No real need for a break here unless you or your dog fancies it. Count out ten more treats.
10. Ask for "it's not" and wait for more pronounced backwards ear motions. Build on intensity first, so only click and treat the ears going back properly.
11. When you have good backwards movement, build on duration - so hold off that click until your dog is holding his ears back and waiting for the click.
12. Now count out ten more treats and alternate between asking for "is it?" and "it's not".

Well done! Isn't this fun? I think it is. My dogs love practising – I hope yours do, too. Remember, always include time for some fun games afterwards. It's like a mental warm down for both of you.

SESSION 5:9: EAR TWITCH ("TWITCH")

What you will need:
- The clicker
- 50 treats
- Two pots
- Yoga space

Learning to recognise your dog's many expressions will help you to understand him.

1. Count out ten treats and have one in your hand ready.
2. Ask for "is it?" Click and treat.
3. Ask for "it's not". Click and treat.
4. Now wait: your dog will offer both the previously rewarded behaviours.
5. Wait until the ears come forward and then back.
6. Click and treat.
7. Wait and repeat, clicking and treating the back/forward motion.
8. Count out ten more treats.
9. Now this time say "twitch".
10. Wait for the ears to go back and then forward.
11. Click and treat.
12. Ask again for "twitch".
13. Wait for two forward/back motions before you click.
14. Now this time three motions, then four, then five.
15. For the remaining five treats, click and reward sporadically. You are looking for your dog to understand that "twitch" cues him to move his ears forwards and then back, until told otherwise via the clicker.
16. Take a break.
17. Count out 20 treats. Remember, as always, that it is not a bad thing to repeat steps if you think your dog is not quite ready to move forward. That might even mean that you stop and try again the next day. There is no time pressure and these exercises are designed to take as long as they take.
18. If your dog has 'got it' then start alternating between "is it?", "it's not" and "twitch" until you run out of treats.

Gosh! What a clever dog you have. It's insane how far you have come from the start of all this training – you guys should feel so proud. Show your dog how delighted you are with cuddles, extra treats and games – whatever he enjoys most – and maybe a race around the garden if it's sunny to finish off!

SESSION 5:10 LOOK AT ME ("WATCH")

This is the last one! Bear in mind that some nervous dogs have a problem with eye contact. It is easy to take for granted that socially sound dogs are good at appropriating their behaviour for us. They would not look at each other with the same direct eye contact that they often make with us. It has always interested me that we have such a strong,

natural desire for eye contact with our dogs, which is quite unnatural for them. That said, we do desire it and, in everyday life, you will look into your dog's eyes to search for a connection. Rather than the unrealistic goal of educating all of humanity not to do this, we are better off teaching our dogs that it's fine and actually quite nice!

What you need:
• Clicker
• 50 treats
• Two pots; an active one and a-non active one
• Yoga space

1. Count out ten treats.
2. Start happy talking to your dog: "Hey buddy, how's it going, what are we up to!" – that kind of thing.
3. As soon as his eyes spring to you, click and treat.
4. Repeat this nine times.
5. Count out ten more treats.
6. Stop the happy talk, sit and wait.
7. Click and treat the eye contact.
8. Repeat this four times.
9. Now start saying "watch", clicking and treating the eye contact by tossing a treat on the floor.
10. Take out the remaining 30 treats and put them in the active pot.
11. Alternate between all ten expressions, including "watch".

That's it – hurray! The journey is not over, but you have now taught all three posture sets, all fifteen actions and ten expressions, which is amazing. You can practise, and chain sequences together as well as taking your training outside the Yoga environment. Well done for completing the basic Dog Yoga programme. Now go and show your dog some loving!

Watch.

SECTION THREE
REAL DOG YOGA FOR DOGS IN CHALLENGING ENVIRONMENTS OR SHOWING CHALLENGING BEHAVIOUR

D ogs are incredible at adapting to new environments. Over the time I have spent with them, I have been dumbfounded by just how quickly they learn new rules, new routines and change their own behaviours in order to thrive.

The domestic world is highly unpredictable and often nonsensical, yet most dogs build a fantastic set of context cues which allows them to predict how to get what they want and what they need. Some dogs live on farms, others in tiny apartments. Some go on trips by plane or on boats and accompany their owners round the world. There are dogs with their own jobs detecting seizures, assisting people with disabilities, searching for drugs or protecting police and army personnel. Our dogs are amazing.

Sometimes, however, we put dogs in more challenging environments, where, more often than not, they are unable to thrive and sometimes fail to cope entirely. These environments are often not permanent for a dog (such as a stay at the vet or time in boarding/rehoming or police kennels), but often the rituals learnt in these contexts – and their trauma – causes subsequent problems when dogs re-enter a 'normal' domestic setting. When dogs cannot manage, and it looks as though they are going to have to be in the situation long term we must, as animal lovers, consider other options.

Common challenging environments for dogs include:
• Shelters
• Police custody
• House arrest
• Veterinary quarantine
• Post operative box rest

These are situations where dogs are unlikely to thrive and many find it hard to cope.

KENNELS

There are many dogs that struggle in shelter kennels, police kennels or boarding kennels. Unfortunately, I have seen dogs go from perfectly rehomable to extremely hard to place in a matter of four frustrating weeks 'inside' these places, despite extensive work by staff to create better environments and routines.

Part of the problem is the lack of social and mental stimulation. Whilst kennel staff may do their absolute best to ensure that kennels are clean, that dogs are fed and walked, it is the lack of engaging social interaction and mental stimulation which, generally, causes dogs to struggle.

The training schedule in this book is designed to create extremely short sessions which should be easy to implement in a kennel environment. Even these sessions can be reduced and cut into smaller sessions – the aim is to reinforce calmness and increase focus. Learning these important skills can really make a difference.

Resulting problems often stem from frustration, but can lead to fearful dogs. Common frustration based problems in kennels are:
• Boundary frustration. This includes fence pacing, barking, frustrated aggressive display on presentation of new dogs, new people, and sometimes known people.
• Over-excitement on the presentation of interaction. This may include jumping up, reactivity on approach, mouthing, pulling at clothes, and vocalisation, which can make it very hard for dogs to be chosen by prospective owners.

Some dogs struggle in a kennel environment.

- Unwanted vocalisation: This takes the form of barking, howling and whining which usually increases with the presence of dogs or people and can escalate to what sounds like aggressive vocalisations.
- Destructiveness: Wrecking toys, beds, blankets, etc.

Common fear-based problems in kennels include:
- Disengagement with people and other dogs: This is generally seen as consistent avoidance which can, sadly, go unnoticed by staff.
- Loss of appetite.
- Low, frightened movements and sometimes hiding from new people.
- Aggression towards new or known people or dogs.
- Guarding behaviours: These may relate to space, resource and food guarding.

Providing a kenneled dog with a clean, stress-free environment to learn behaviours, which are intrinsically relaxing as well as rewarding, can make a huge difference. With dogs who are struggling in kennels, this kind of learning can encourage desirable behaviour and help build a better more positive outlook overall.

SOMETHING TO TRY...
Tie a clicker to the kennel where staff, volunteers and (if it is an open kennel) the public pass. Put the dog's dry dinner portion in a container clipped to the kennel. Print and display one of the postures, with an explanation, for example asking passers to: "click and throw one piece of food into Cassie's kennel if she is in a settle".

By doing this sort of training we are continually stimulating the dog, as well as rewarding behaviour which is appropriate. Dogs are also learning what postures are most rewarding in the presence of people. For scardy dogs, try rewarding soft eyes, look aways, settles, as well as paw raises. Put a description, a photo and an explanation on the printout.

Additionally, you will find that by teaching dogs to sit quietly when people come through kennels (see the tips for dogs on kennel arrested and quarantine below), you can dramatically reduce frustration and the associated problems. This is also true in rescue kennels, and this reformed behaviour can significantly improve the chance of potential adopters being interested in a dog.

A fun and positive challenge for a kennel manager is to allocate a dog to each member of staff, and they must be in charge of teaching their dog to do a trick as soon as he sees someone. The cue is a person walking into the kennels and, on this context cue, the dog should present his posture. I am pretty sure that the Jack Russell Terrier who salutes potential adopters with a paw raise is more likely to be adopted than the one that barks and tail chases when anyone comes past!

POST OPERATIVE
How do you keep a seven-month-old Vizsla from moving too much? No, this is not the punchline of a doggy joke. It is a serious question that is posed all too often. A vet has to keep the physical well-being of his/her patient as the number one priority, but

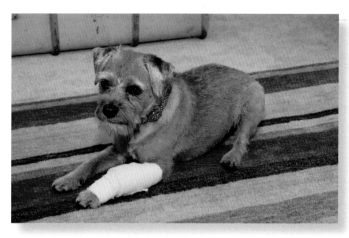

Yoga can help dogs post surgery.

holding enhances muscle control and promotes healing.

Look through the postures and decide which ones you would like to teach your dog. I would suggest showing these to your vet and checking that none of the stretches or movements involved are likely to put pressure on the area which the dog has had investigated. In fact, the best way to see whether a posture is comfortable or not, is to watch your dog. Check that he is getting into the position readily and ensure that there are no signs of stress or discomfort. If your dog is struggling with a position after he has had surgery, your best bet is to leave it and try a different position.

keeping Fido from eating his stitches and from jumping on and off the sofa when he is getting no walks can be nearly impossible!

Dogs who have had to endure surgery, even when it is something as simple as castration, get frustrated without their usual exercise. A lot of this is about expectation. Dogs come to expect a certain level of energy to be expelled every day and when suddenly these needs are not met, it inevitably and understandably causes feelings of frustration. Fido will look for a way to get rid of this energy – zooming around the garden or chewing a pair of shoes. Dog Yoga exercises are perfect for post-op dogs who are on 'box rest'. The physical stretches and actions require muscle control and exercise the dog in a base way, which does not promote high arousal or include anything rigorous or physically risky. You will also find that these short exercises tire your dog out, too. Clicker training mentally stimulates a dog to a point where he becomes tired but, additionally, the stretching and

KENNEL ARREST AND QUARANTINE

Unfortunately, it is the case that some dogs and puppies, due to illness (such as parvovirus) or due to being defined as illegal or dangerous, have to be kept in a kennel in isolation. These cases are perhaps some of the saddest I have seen. Without any level of real human or dog-to-dog interaction, little or no physical contact or mental stimulation, let alone physical stimulation, these dogs suffer an unspeakable torture.

I would like to note that, I personally, feel that there are no circumstances that warrant a

Engaging in Yoga can be of real benefit to a dog in isolation giving him much-needed mental stimulation.

dog being kept in isolation. I think that putting a dog to sleep in these situations is kinder. It has been my experience that some kennels that look after illegal or supposedly dangerous dogs for the police, are, on occasion, asked not to allow the dogs out of their enclosures. I have visited kennels where frustrated Bull Terriers are literally leaping at the fences – barking and growling and hurting themselves on the mesh that is the boundary between themselves and the 'real world'. This is the kind of torture we use as punishments for the most hideous human crimes, such as rape and murder. There are no dogs who deserve to live in these conditions.

In these situations where dogs, albeit through fear of the spread of disease or unjust legal processing, have to endure long periods of being locked away, they should be provided with opportunities to engage with humans and to influence their own environment. You can train a dog, using the above methods, without touching the dog through the bars of

a cage. Using the optional shaping methods (described above), there is no reason why a dog in kennels, imprisoned in a cage for hours, cannot at least enjoy a level of engagement. This will lead to a more positive connection with the outside world, and he will learn important lessons which will help him to make good decisions, cope better and avoid frustration.

For some dogs, the simple process of loading the clicker – clicking and treating repeatedly so that the dog understands that the noise means a treat is on its way – is too much. For these dogs eye contact, in fact the very presence of a person they cannot interact with physically, can cause frustration or fear. As is usual with frustration and fear, proximity is key. To understand this we need to revisit the idea of the ideal training situ for the dog being further back that we, as humans, think is necessary. This notion (discussed in *Things to do before you train to reduce tension and stress*, on page 18), highlights the need to observe a dog to see how far away you need to be. If he is barking or growling, giving appeasement or avoidance; if he is unable to eat, listen or engage, then the first thing to do is add distance. How much distance depends on the dog. We must give our dogs a voice, a say in what they are learning and how they are learning.

Distance is the first step. We move away until the dog opts in. For some dogs this is cued with a change of posture; some will take a step forward towards us, as if to say "far enough". A dog cannot speak but he is talking all the time, so listen closely! In these abnormal circumstances, it is not surprising that our training must be adjusted, too. We must listen harder for signs that a dog wants to opt out, or that he isn't coping. Additionally, it is extremely important to reward desirable behaviour in this unnatural setting. You can do this easily, and the first few sessions you should focus on very slow, very straightforward postures: sit, down and stand. During the learning process mark and reward focus, engagement and soft eyes, particularly while working on duration and increasing patience. Work on shaping out any ritualised vocalisations, but if vocalisation is frequent then you are asking too much. Slow the session down further, perhaps simply click and treat micro-seconds of quiet or quieter vocalisation, eye contact, attention or (where fixation is a problem), the drop of a gaze.

For dogs who are staying in kennels for a long period of time, the presence of people can cause much frustration. Counter-condition this and reward appropriate responses in this context. To do this you can simply appear in the kennel, mark and reward, and then disappear. Repeat this and then chain a sit into the ritual. Walk in front of the kennel, ask for a "sit", mark and treat, disappear and repeat. After you have practised this frequently, you can begin holding back and not asking for the sit. Simply walk in, wait and mark and reward the decision on the dog's part to sit. Repeat this and practise it with the other dogs in the kennels, too, as well as using other people in kennels as stooges so that the dogs learn to generalise the behaviour.

Frustration is remarkably contagious. It spreads like wildfire from dog to dog and from dog to handler. Work with the most frustrated dog in the kennels first, and then work down the line. There is nothing better than walking down a line of quiet, relaxed dogs who come out to greet people, expectantly, and sit calmly.

DEFINING A DOG SHOWING CHALLENGING BEHAVIOUR

Trainers and behaviourists used to believe that dogs exhibiting challenging behaviour were dogs that tried to challenge us. This is an old and, frankly illogical, theory based on an over-simplistic, supposed linear hierarchy structure in wolves. It created a monstrous industry which used fear and pain to force dogs into a state the trainer called submissive.

These days, scientifically qualified or experienced behaviourists understand that a problem is only a problem to someone who finds it so. By that I mean that some people find their dog barking at new people at the door problematic, and some find it reassuring.

Defining a dog showing challenging behaviour: Ella in the van.

A dog who barks at new people coming to the door is, therefore, only a problem if the caregiver defines him so. For the purpose of this book, I am looking at challenging dogs as opposed to problem dogs. A challenging dog is a dog whose behaviour is not usual in a given situation and, as such, it is sometimes considered a problem to the caregiver, and sometimes not.

In my experience, the vast majority of challenging behaviour is prompted by an emotional response to a specific situation or set of circumstances. When a dog is presented to us as being "challenging", the first port of call is to ensure that a vet has given him a clean bill of health. Pain, and other physical and neurological abnormalities, have such huge implications on behaviour; it is, therefore, of paramount importance that a dog is given the all clear before any training or behaviour modification is considered.

If a dog is physically healthy – but presenting with abnormal behaviours – it is my belief that these behaviours are, nearly always, the result of fear, frustration, or a combination of both.

A simple way to think about fear and frustration is to suppose that fear is having what you don't want, and frustration is not having what you do want.

It is then only natural that fear based behaviours are usually proximity increasers. That is, the dog does whatever moves the thing he is frightened of away. This would infer when frustrated, a dog will do what moves the object of frustration (or the 'trigger' object, context or being that brings about an emotional response which causes a behaviour change) closer to the dog. It is important to note that this is not actually the case. Frustration behaviour also increases proximity (space between the dog and the trigger), which is why it can be hard for the average owner to see if a dog is frightened or if he is frustrated, when you merely observe a dog after they have changed their behaviour towards the trigger.

When a trigger frequently causes a dog to feel frustration, the dog will look to remove himself (avoidance) from the trigger or to make the trigger move away (appeasement escalating to conflict). What this means is that to an owner, a dog's behaviour when the dog is frightened often looks similar to his behaviour when he is frustrated. Then it is only common sense that we, again, slow the process down, and look at behaviour towards a trigger before they have a significant emotional response to it in order to realise the functional goal of the dog in any given context. Ultimately this means giving your dog a voice as well as looking at what function the reaction to the trigger serves. By doing this we can observe that both feelings of fear as well as frustration towards a trigger can cause a dog to behave in a way which serves the function of eliminating a trigger.

To prevent fear and frustration occurring we must look to keep a dog 'under threshold' at all times. That means that when we are working with the trigger of fear and frustration we have to work with enough distance from it so as to ensure the dog feels comfortable. This is possible, and Dog Yoga can be extremely useful in reducing fear and frustration overall, as well as reducing fear and frustration caused by a trigger. The key here is to remember that in everyday situations we must help our dogs to make good choices. This shies away from command-based training and, instead, looks at teaching a dog what to do and then reinforcing his choice to do it. The aim of training fearful and frustrated dogs should not then be people-led. It needs to be dog-led.

FRUSTRATION

CAUSES

Most frustrated behaviour serves the function of getting rid of energy, and so it is with energy in mind that we must look at

Poor behaviour can be a sign of excess energy or frustration.

what causes frustration. It comes when an expectation is not met. A dog is ready (and actively energised) for a situation which then does not occur. The word frustration comes from the Latin *frustratio,* meaning disappointment.

While there are obvious physical consequences of frustration, it is frustration as a feeling, an emotion, that we are looking at here. The science of canine behaviour has manoeuvred gently around the idea of canine emotions for some time now. As in human psychology, scientists felt more comfortable looking at what comes out of the 'black box', rather than guessing what happens inside it. However, as technology and training has improved, so has our ability to study, scientifically, hormone release and brain activity in dogs. It seems the industry is now finally able to accept the cognitive and emotional side of dogs more freely.

Of course, no dog owner needs graphs and data to prove that a dog feels loved when he is petted. Although, interestingly, studies have substantiated these observations by looking at how dogs release oxytocin when they are petted and, in just the same way as when a person feels love or loved, their caudate nucleus is activated when they are petted, too. However, even if dogs are releasing the same hormones and using the same parts of their brain as us in specific contexts, do they still feel the same? Dogs have eyes and so do humans, but the world looks very different. I suppose the important thing to consider is the way that the behaviour reflects the emotion. In terms of frustration, I would hypothesise

that dogs, in terms of brain functions and hormone release but, most importantly, in terms of feelings, experience a similar frustration to us. I base this on their behaviour displays in contexts where frustration is being experienced.

When a dog is frustrated by an object, his outward behaviour is similar to our own. He wants to, and often does, break things. This may not always be the object of frustration, sometimes it may be something else. In this situation, a dog will vocalise in long, whiney tones as we do. He will look long and hard at the object, and posture in a staccato and irritated manner – just as we do.

For example, imagine a dog who has prepared to play with another dog he has seen across the street. He gets himself ready for the play: tensing his muscles (in preparation to run), and releasing hormones such as adrenaline. He is, however, on the road, on a lead, and so is his buddy. Fido usually gets to play with his buddy and he has prepared himself physically. He feels frustrated. He has energy and it has nowhere to go. So what happens to the energy?

Some dogs are excellent at de-escalating from a frustrated state; they will simply shake off and move forward, accepting this disappointment is an inevitable part of life. Some are not so accepting. There are many, many factors that influence how dogs dispel this unneeded energy, but all dogs feel frustration to some degree, in their daily life. Expectation is, if you like, the cause of frustration. With this in mind, we should raise a puppy to understand that disappointment is inevitable, so he has realistic expectations.

There are specific environments and situations which actively seem to cause frustration. Most commonly, these include:

• Not enough physical exercise.
• Not enough mental stimulation.
• Not enough social stimulation.
• Games with no gratifying reward (the best example I can think of is a game with a Boomer Ball – these are massive balls that dogs chase and chase but cannot chew, pick up or get their teeth into).
• Food which is visible but the dog cannot reach.
• Being on lead around dogs in a context where off-lead play is usual.
• A boundary/barrier between a dog and something of interest.
• Small, fast, furry animals, such as squirrels, which cannot be caught.

Of course, for many dogs, just being asked to sit still is frustrating!

SYMPTOMS OF FRUSTRATION

As suggested above, frustration is a part of life. It is just another stressor and, as caregivers, it is not possible to eliminate all stress from the lives of our canine companions. However, it is our job to try to ensure that this type of 'normal' stress is manageable. We can manage the environment to reduce this type of stress by ensuring our dogs' needs are met. Tidying up the environment of unnecessary stress is helpful, but it is equally important to is teach dogs to manage their own feelings.

When dogs become frustrated their behavioural output is not dissimilar to our own. Stress signals (from nose licking, head turning and pawing to panting, growling and even biting), breaking things (active destruction often pointed at the object of frustration but also sometimes redirected), movement and weight forward, fixation behaviours (staring, hard eyes, inability to move away or look away from the trigger), unintentional self-harming and increasing arousal, are all indicative of frustration. I have heard owners describe their dogs as "angry", suggesting "he just sees red".

COMMON RESULTING PROBLEMS

There are lots of problems which stem from frustration. They include:

• Destructiveness.
• Separation anxiety.
• Unwanted barking.
• Behaviour which is described as "attention seeking".
• Car/bike/child chasing.
• On lead reactivity.
• Dog-to-dog aggression.
• Human aggression.

Physically speaking, too much stress is not good for your dog's health, but behaviourally I would suggest that problems stemming from frustration are also one of the largest cause for rehoming dogs.

FEAR

SYMPTOMS OF FEAR

Fear is, in my experience, one of the most misunderstood and common causes for behaviour problems in domestic dogs. Fear is defined as the emotion caused by a perceived threat. As with frustration, I find it is most useful looking at the behavioural output caused by this type of stress when we are looking for ways to help our dogs.

Fear is an incredibly important survival adaptation. It is needed. If dogs didn't feel frightened they would be eaten by other animals, hit by cars and killed by people. However, often due to trauma, a caregiver's ignorance or a lack of exposure to something commonplace, a dog may become fearful of a trigger which they have to deal with frequently. Again, the concept of stored energy is a useful

way to think about fear. Like frustration, there is an increase of energy inside a dog when he perceives a threat. He then uses that energy to partake in behaviours which he sees as successful in reducing the threat. Broadly speaking, these behaviours are either avoidance based (flight, hiding or care solicitation), proximity increasing behaviours (space negotiation, barking, growling, lunging, biting), or sometimes, when a dog feels he has no other choice, confrontational behaviours (fight). All these types of behaviour are an attempt to reduce the threat by getting distance from it, or killing it. While aggression is frightening for an animal caregiver to witness, it is important that we recognise its functionality in the context of fear. Dogs are emotionally complex and sensitive, and they have to live in our domestic world. It is our responsibility to help dogs to interpret that world so as to reduce the incidence of incorrect perception of threat.

Fear is one of the most unrecognised causes of behavioural problems in dogs.

THE REAL DOG YOGA

The behaviour output from this kind of stress begins with proximity increase (where possible), which includes running away, hiding and cowering, appeasement and passive suggestive communication signals such as yawning, looking away, nose licking and paw lifting, and then more active communication signals, such as barking, growling and biting.

COMMON RESULTING PROBLEMS

There are many problems which occur as a result of fear including but not exclusive to:

• Generalised anxiety.
• Fear of new things (neophobia).
• Disengagement under pressure.
• Hiding from triggers.
• Significant stress towards triggers.
• Unwanted barking.
• Aggression towards new people.
• Aggression towards new dogs.
• Aggression towards all people.
• Aggression towards all dogs.

REDUCING FEAR AND FRUSTRATION WITH DOG YOGA

As I wrote in my introduction, Archie was my muse for this method of training. Archie is the most frustrated dog I have ever had the pleasure of working with. He is a registered Pit Bull Terrier. I would suggest, perhaps controversially, that the UK version of this breed is predisposed to high arousal which is often reflected in feelings of frustration. There are many reasons for this, but this book is not the place to go into detail. I have

worked with lots of British Pit Bulls; they all suffer with frustration and high arousal to some degree, and that this is a large cause of them getting into so much trouble! Archie, when I first bought him home, was a very frustrated chap.

THE IMPORTANCE OF THRESHOLD

Threshold, in this context, is simply the space required from a trigger in order to practise normal behaviour. One of the main reasons why it is important to seek the help of professionals when working with fearful and frustrated dogs is that a dog's emotional threshold to a trigger is in a constant state of flux, which is sometimes hard to spot, and is one of the most important things to get right.

The trigger for proximity increasing behaviour – be that avoidance, appeasement or conflict – reduces with distance. There are other factors which affect the intensity of a trigger but I think distance is often the easiest and most successful variable to work with. The more intense a trigger appears, i.e. the more frustrating or scary it is, the more distance a dog needs from it before he can regulate himself physically and feel normal enough to participate in something as challenging as facilitated learning.

There are things we can then do to help a dog who has unpleasant emotional responses, such as feeling scared or frustrated, when confronted with specific things or situations:

• Teach behaviours and techniques in a clean environment without triggers present before practising them with triggers present.

- Give these behaviours verbal cues so that we can ask a dog to participate in a challenging environment. This makes it clear what will be rewarding. Only when a dog understands what prompts a reward, can we give him the space to chose to participate or not.
- Be extremely aware of the distance a dog may require from a trigger before he feels able to practise learnt behaviours and take non participation as a sign of struggle, not a sign of defiance.
- When working with frightened or frustrated dogs everything needs to be slower. Doing nothing is not doing nothing – it is processing. If a dog needs time to look, to listen, to scent, to think, give it to him. It is as much part of the learning process as engaging in learnt behaviours.

So to be clear: when working with fearful or frustrated dogs it is important that they never practise proximity increasing behaviours. If a dog is practising behaviours which aim to increase proximity (avoidance, appeasement, confrontation or conflict) then we are over threshold. Again, this is about both the human and the dog in the partnership. A dog over threshold is a human over threshold, and vice-versa.

WHAT CAN WE DO TO STOP A DOG FEELING UNHEALTHY FRUSTRATION OR FEAR?

1. We can accept that there are too many normal things that act as triggers for frustration or fear, and that the daily life for the dog is unpleasant. In these cases we must look at rehoming to an environment with less triggers, or consider euthanasia.
2. We can manage the environment to reduce stimuli that may cause frustration or fear. For example, avoiding other dogs while our dog is on the lead out on walks, or keeping our dog in a different room when kids are playing chase games in the garden.
3. We can, over time, work to change the dog's emotional response to stimuli that cause frustration or fear he has to experience in everyday life. This can be done using Behaviour Adjustment Training, counter conditioning, desensitization, plus similar functional reward programmes to teach the dog that a calm and communicative response gets him what he wants, and that the trigger is actually neither scary nor frustrating.
4. We can teach our dogs to manage their feelings appropriately and to use posture, expression and action to de-escalate themselves proactively in order to reduce arousal and unwanted energy.

All four of the above approaches can be entirely appropriate, although I would suggest that commonly, 2, 3 and 4 can be used together in the vast majority of cases for the best effect.

TREATMENT

In my opinion, fear and frustration can be greatly reduced using Dog Yoga, not merely as a distraction, but as a way of actively reinforcing and teaching de-escalation techniques. Teaching a frustrated or frightened dog to calm himself in situations where he feels stressed increases processing. This allows a dog to enter an otherwise arousing environment and analyse more rationally what will be functional. This just means that, for example, Alfie can learn to self soothe when he sees another dog and keep his own arousal down. He, therefore, remains able to process the behaviour of the oncoming dog and make better decisions without high arousal causing an escalated response.

Cueing a de-escalation set of postures, actions and expressions, and then reinforcing this set around objects of frustration or fear, greatly improves a dog's ability to systematically de-escalate around tricky environments and around objects which we cannot control. We can also improve impulse control and generally reduce frustration and fear simply by practicing Dog Yoga itself, which sets out to reinforce calmness and stillness and increase confidence and human engagement.

HOW DOES THIS WORK EXACTLY...

Along with daily Dog Yoga practised regularly to ensure that our dogs are mentally stimulated and are being challenged and rewarded for desirable choices, we can specifically use cued sequences which de-escalate dogs. The de-escalation sequence (as laid out below) can be used in two ways to help prevent and also to change frustrated and fearful behaviours.

The first tip is to practise the sequence to prevent a dog entering a situation in an aroused state. A good example of this is a dog who suffer with lead reactivity on walks. Irrespective of the trigger (bikes, cars, other dogs), once a ritual of behaviour has developed by repeated experiences of frustration or fear on lead walks, precursory events cause arousal to increase before the event. What I mean by this is at when Alfie (who is frustrated by other dogs) goes for his walkies, before he leaves the door his energy already increases. Clues (shoes on, lead on etc) tell Alfie that he is about to go into a predictable context where frustration is likely. His expectation causes him to practise frustrated output before he even leaves the door. In other words Alfie's vocalisation, rushing behaviours, muscle tension and general energy (which is also his response to triggers) starts being practised, albeit on a low level, before he leaves the house!

Some trainers try asking caregivers to change the routine or to practise the leaving routine (shoes on, lead on etc.) without actually going out. However, I personally find these sort of unpractical methods are hard to practise sensibly and also have little real effect (dogs are very aware of real intention. Yep – they usually know when we're trying to trick them). Instead, using the de-escalation sequence we can bring a dog's energy down before they go out (or just before they are left in cases of separation anxiety). They are then entering a situation in a lowered state of arousal. We can repeat this before frustrated greeters enter a park and before frustrated agility dogs enter the ring, as well as while they are waiting for their go (this has been extremely useful in improving accuracy in flyball with dogs that suffer with attention problems as a result of being distracted by other teams running while they are waiting). It is also useful before scared dogs are asked to walk near a busy road or enter a hall with people or other dogs in it. We can also mark and reward active de-escalation in these situation, clicking shake-offs, yawns, ground sniffing and anything else which sets to defuse and de-escalate.

The second way we can use Dog Yoga is to ask a dog to practise a set of previously-learnt de-escalation postures around a trigger – but under threshold. This, of course, requires the help of a professional. This is because an exceptionally accurate measurement of emotional threshold is needed in order to ensure the dog is not being stressed further by the treatment.

The emotional threshold we are talking about in these cases refers to the dog's ability to tolerate the object of frustration or fear.

To give a personal example of using this treatment I will go back to my insanely frustrated Pit Bull. Objects which caused Archie immense frustration were sticks. As he is a registered Pit Bull, he has to wear a muzzle on walks and being that he is Bull Terrier he has no greater joy than carrying things his mouth. Before he was muzzled (and before me), I would imagine his owners played with him a lot on walks with sticks. He is drawn to them like a moth to a flame. They cause him immense frustration, though as he is unable to get them through his muzzle. He would see a stick out on a walk and immediately become aroused. His coat would bristle and his muscles would tense. He would whine and then dart at the

stick trying to get it through his muzzle in a fixated fashion until I physically had to remove him from the situation by picking him up. This is one of the situations where no amount of recall practice seemed to help. So, this trigger was not enough for me to consider rehoming or euthanasia. I could avoid sticks but that would be extremely hard, given that I live in the countryside. So instead I decided to work with this frustrated fixation.

I first taught Arch a set of de-escalating postures at home and chained them. On entering the areas where he frequently found sticks, I started practising the sequence before we went in. This reduced the frequency of stick obsession (around a quarter of the sticks we saw on the walk would trigger a response as opposed to three-quarters) but didn't entirely stop it.

I began to practise the sequence as soon as I noticed his body begin to change. In this way he was under threshold – just. He was aware of the trigger but had not reacted to the stick, and his arousal was not high enough to stop him from being able to participate in normal behaviours, or to listen to me. Over a few days of practising this, I noticed not only were we moving much closer to the sticks before his body was changing (i.e. his frustration aimed towards the object was decreasing), but he also began to practise the postures on his own (self soothing) more proactively. When given the choice, I was surprised to see Arch choosing to stay calm and actively learning to reduce his own arousal.

The key to using the sequence around triggers is to keep dogs below their emotional threshold all the time. Working out where your dog's thresholds are is complex and depends, broadly, on the strength of the trigger, the position of the trigger, the perceived value of reward, how practised the sequence is, the environment and the competency of the handler, as well as things like the temperature, light and shade, the likelihood that other triggers may occur in this context and scent from the trigger, the environment and the handler. This is why owners should seek the help of a professional to teach them how to practise the technique safely – particularly if the frustration or fear has led to intense behaviour outcomes in the past.

ARCHIE'S SEQUENCE OF DE-ESCALATION

- Sit
- Front right paw raise
- Front left paw raise
- Stretch left
- Stretch right
- Turn left
- Turn right
- Stand
- Stretch left
- Stretch right
- Standing right paw raise
- Standing left paw raise
- For four
- Shake
- For four
- Then proceed toward trigger

This sequence depends, of course, on what behaviours your dog uses to de-escalate.

Different dogs have different sequences to self sooth and to calm themselves. Ralph the Bull Terrier likes nothing better than to destress by rolling around on the floor – so we include rolling in his de-escalating set. To work out the right set of behaviours/ for your dog you need to analyse how he relaxes. The postures, expressions and actions should be ones he enjoys practising and, so long as you are under threshold there is no reason why your dog should struggle to practise.

"STUBBORN," "DOMINANT" OR "NAUGHTY" DOGS THAT DON'T LISTEN

I can honestly, hand on heart, say that I have never met a "stubborn" dog. There are dogs who find it hard to focus and dogs that find conventional training pressurising and confrontational as well as a host of other emotional and physical reasons that makes complying with a specific command difficult.

Real Dog Yoga is all about development of a physical dialogue between you and your dog. Optional clicker training sessions improve a dog's work ethic and empower him so as to increase the desirability of training sessions for him. The environment for learning reduces distractions and the specific criteria and increased clarity of what and how you are training postures, ensures that training is made easy, calming, non-pressured and fun for dogs.

Try this. Get your clicker and your treats. For three days spend five minutes a day in the Yoga space. Sit on the floor. Click and reward the following: dog entering the room, dog sitting by you, dog lying down near you, dog looking at you, dog touching you. Every time your dog does an action on the list, click and treat. For five minutes for three days. Then start teaching the postures. Remember to keep calm, respect your dog's attention span and to go back and repeat this step if your dog begins to opt out readily.

Disengagement is a sign of struggle, not of defiance. Purposeful defiance is not functional or adaptive for a dog, which is why I have never seen it practised. Appreciate your dog for the beautifully functional and wonderfully social being he is. If he is struggling to learn, first look at the environment, then the lesson, then the reward, then yourself.

Enjoy your dog for the wonderful animal he is.

ABOUT THE AUTHOR

Jo-Rosie Haffenden is a dog behaviorist and runs her own Behaviour Centre in Sussex. She has a degree in psychology and advanced post graduate qualifications in canine psychology, specialising in aggression. She is a fully accredited member of the Institute of Modern Dog Trainers (IMDT) and a fully accredited behaviourist for The Professional Pet Guild which is the association of force-free training and behaviour. As well as being the recommended behaviourist for various animal rescue centres, Jo-Rosie also works as an approved expert witness for the courts in dangerous dog cases.

In her spare time, Jo-Rosie uses her own dogs (including her exempt Pit Bull Terrier) and her Bengal cat for TV and filming work with animals having featured in *Vogue* magazine, *Cosmopolitan*, *Topshop*, *GQ* magazine as well as adverts and drama series' for the BBC, Channel 4 and ITV.